CHASING EXCELLENCE

Real Life Stories from the Streets

Bill Lee | **R. Craig Coppola**

Founder – Lee & Associates | #1 Producer – Lee & Associates

COMMERCIAL REAL ESTATE

This publication is designed to provide competent and reliable information regarding the subject matter covered. However, it is sold with the understanding that the author and publisher are not engaged in rendering accounting, architectural, financial, legal, real estate, or other professional advice. Laws and practices often vary from state to state and country to country and if legal or other expert assistance is required, the services of a professional should be sought. The author and publisher specifically disclaim any liability that is incurred from the use or application of the contents of this book.

Published by:
Lee IV, LLC • 190 Sea Wind Way, Los Osos, CA 93402
and
Habanero Publishing LLC • 6040 E Montecito Ave • Scottsdale, AZ 85251

Printed in the United States of America

First Edition: 2016

ISBN 978-1517459802

ACKNOWLEDGEMENTS

Thank you to those original partners who joined, believed, and created Lee & Associates with me, and thank you to the many who follow to this day, perpetuating a corporate democracy like no other.

Bill Lee

Thanks to Bill for the opportunity to help open the Lee & Associates Arizona in 1991. Since then he has been a mentor and friend. Thanks to my wife, Tracy, who allows me to pursue excellence and thank you to my team who chase excellence every single day.

R. Craig Coppola

Thank you also to Kellie Coppola, for her diligence in helping us write this book, and to Kathy Heasley for her direction and guidance.

Bill and Craig

CONTENTS

72   Section III: Refine Excellence

FOREWORD

When Bill Lee started Lee & Associates in 1979, he and his original partners had a limited perspective of the company's future potential. They could not foresee the thousands of lives they would change by giving brokers, present and future, a chance to chase excellence on their own terms.

Excellence, self-actualization, accomplishment, productivity; they are all brothers and sisters in the world of becoming as good as you can be and that is what this book is about.

In this book, Bill and Craig not only include their own lessons, stories, and wisdom, but also collect experiences from multiple brokers who have carved their own path to the top. They examine the journey honestly, acknowledging the difficulties as well as the rewards of a life chasing excellence. Those within and outside the commercial real estate business alike will find the content in these pages invaluable to the success of all their future endeavors.

Whether you are a person who is chasing excellence, a person who is content, or even a person who is fooling yourself into thinking you are content, this book will reignite your desire to win and your passion for excellence, and show you how it's done by the people who have done it best.

— Larry Harmsen, COO Americas, Prologis

PREFACE

Bill Lee

My career in commercial real estate (CRE) spans close to forty-five years and in those years, living entirely in California, I've witnessed the population base grow from 20,000,000 to 40,000,000, representing a one-hundred percent increase and making for the most populated state in the Union. I would expect, then, that the office base inventory, industrial base inventory, and the retail base inventory have all grown at significantly greater factors. My personal business focus, industrial real estate in Southern California, has grown to amass almost two billion square feet of space, representing the largest sector base inventory in the United States and probably the world.

As an entry-level salesperson at the Grubb and Ellis Company (G&E) in 1971, I watched my peers in the early years and, of course, noticed their work habits; hours on the job, productivity, priority, focus, mannerisms, communications and the like. These are the qualities that new salespeople note from those working around them with experience.

Nine years later, in 1979, after experiencing success at G&E, I brought together a group of partners to form Lee & Associates with the goal of creating a unique commercial real estate brokerage company. The concept was that by creating an entity that dispersed profits to the salespeople in the same percentage that gross revenue was brought in by these same salespeople, and at the same time giving these salespeople an equal vote in ownership, we would create an environment of sharing such that it would promote greater productivity for all; salespeople, clients, and all those who would participate in the future.

Over the next thirty-six years, I watched the organization grow to today having fifty-four locations and nine hundred salespeople across the United States. And in that time, I've come to know a sampling of more than a thousand brokers personally. This includes a large segment of the Lee & Associates brokers, as well as countless others in different offices, markets, states, even countries and within our competitors.

The brokers whom I've met and formed relationships with represent all types of salespeople; some willing to do whatever it took to be successful and others unwilling to pay the price for the same success. They range from runners to senior executives and owners, with different backgrounds, education, and personalities. Some succeeded, some failed, and an overwhelming majority were content to exist in their own world, which I will call "reactionary brokerage."

However, there was and continues to be, a select group of professionals who, year after year, perform at levels far higher than the average commercial real estate professional. The individuals in this group achieve at a level of excellence that sets them apart from their peers. They seem able to continually maintain their excellence in spite of a market of ever-changing conditions.

Furthermore, these professionals don't seem as harried as the average practitioner. They wear a smile and have a peace about them, walk with self-assuredness, always seem organized and prepared, don't seem to spend that many more work hours than their peers, and generally seem to have a very balanced life.

Like most people, I was focused on myself and my own brand of professionalism in my early years, and I viewed other successful brokers as competitors, as I matured in the industry. I noted varying characteristics of my competitors but I didn't study them or analyze their strengths and weaknesses. In fact, I didn't really take the time to analyze my own strengths and weaknesses and measure myself against them.

The "tools" used by successful professionals vary; some bring enormous energy and effort, some are more organized and prepared, some are more thoughtful and calculating, some bring vision and wisdom, some are more historical and some are more opportunistic, and some seek relationships while others focus on the deal at hand. The key, however, to those who really self-actualize, and seek to continually push their accomplishments to the limits, is the degree to which they implement these tools with thought, organization, preparation, discipline and execution.

In this book, we'll attempt to analyze these individuals and the excellence that they represent, breaking down their various methods so that others might have the chance to follow in their steps. With my partner, Craig Coppola, a shining example of brokerage excellence, we'll dive into the idea of excellence and attempt to flesh out what that accolade truly means.

PREFACE

R. Craig Coppola

In 1991, I was a full-time broker in grad school earning my MBA, my wife, Tracy, was pregnant with our first child, and I was meeting with Bill Lee to form the nucleus to start Lee & Associates Arizona. A busy time to start a company.

Despite my hectic schedule, the choice to leave my current company to help start the Arizona office was the best decision of my business life. Since we began, I have been fortunate to learn from the best – on the streets, with guidance every day from people like Bill Gosnell, Jim Watkins, Bill Blake and my other partners at Lee & Associates. Along the way, my brokerage relationship with Bill Lee deepened and I can now say I have been blessed to really know what excellence looks like in this incredible man.

I enjoyed my own excellence in the years since I started at Lee & Associates. But for me, it was never enough to simply achieve for myself. I am a father, coach, and mentor, dedicated to passing on the lessons I've learned the hard way to help others find their path.

This book is our tangible guide to helping you become the best you can be. You have the potential to improve, win, succeed, and build the life you've always wanted.

INTRODUCTION

We have a choice for most everything we do. Do we just get it done or do we get it done the right way? Most of the time this choice is impacted by the time we have available to do it. Some matters are essential and important; others, not so much. But when it comes to our business career and our lifestyle, the choice to "do it right" separates the pack.

The path to accomplishment in Commercial Real Estate is similar to that in sports. Those who master the fundamentals are ready to take the next step. In sports, success can be measured by acclaim; all-league, all-star, scholarships, and on to a new level of competition. Commercial real estate success often seems to bring with it a new level of competition against the best for the bigger assignments, or it can be for control of larger listings in the market, or for significant investment sales.

If you've picked up this book, odds are you are curious about others' success, or maybe have a desire to improve your own game. Maybe you've seen other practitioners move ahead year after year, and now you want to discover their secrets. Whether you believe you have it in you or not, you know that you have more to give.

The first thing you should know is that you *do* have it in you. In sports, limitations exist that render a "chosen few" above the rest of us. Height, speed, strength, dexterity, and more, are among the assets that separate some from the norm. But in commercial real estate, there are no physical requirements holding you back. You might moan and complain about market conditions, recessions, legal issues, financing, or other outside conditions that you believe are impeding you. But the truth is you have the ability to overcome those external obstacles by mastering the internal.

There are so many ingredients for success and excellence that what may work for one broker, in one market, may not work for another somewhere else. Therefore, chasing excellence becomes more of a mental journey, one that pertains to thought and priority combined with effort, initiative, and desire that give all the participants a chance to reach the top of their chosen profession in their area of expertise and in their chosen geographic area.

This book will help you understand that excellence is always in constant motion. Chasing excellence is a journey that never ends. Your definition of excellence, your goals, your focus, will always change. You must focus your thoughts on your priorities, letting your vision of the future be your guide along the highway of excellence.

PLATFORM PROFILES
Bill Lee

In this book, you'll read the stories of several notable brokers who have chased excellence in varying ways throughout their careers and personal lives. In addition to the stories folded into these chapters, I have also selected a few "extra" notable people and the platforms through which they operate, that I wish to highlight in "Platform Profiles." These are scattered throughout the book, and recognize salespeople from a variety of backgrounds and companies who, despite their differences, have all carved out an incredible level of success for themselves.

Through these Platform Profiles, I wish to highlight not only these outstanding brokers—my nominations for the sadly nonexistent Commercial Real Estate Hall of Fame—but also draw attention to the different platforms and organizations that allow them their success.

PLATFORM PROFILE
R. Craig Coppola (Lee & Associates)

Since Craig is my co-author and partner in this endeavor, it seems only fitting that I begin these Platform Profiles with him. You'll learn a lot more about him in the next few chapters, but this is my summary of why Craig deserves an extra shout-out.

Craig started his real estate career at the Grubb & Ellis Company shortly after he stopped playing professional baseball in The Minnesota Twins organization. He immediately set his sights on chasing excellence in Commercial Real Estate. He was one of the founding shareholders in the formation of the Lee & Associates Arizona office in 1991. He is the all-time money earner in the national Lee & Associates organization and senior partner of the recently-voted #1 Commercial Real Estate sales team in the United States, primarily focused on office sales and leasing.

He is a master of how to pack it all into a lifetime. An author, backpacker, International Tae Kwon Do Hall of Fame member, spouse, father, traveler, mentor, and so much more. He is still going strong at 54 and looking for more to pursue. He is an inspiration to be around and a mentor for me on thinking, process, organization, and living. He is a devoted family man intimately involved in the lives of his four children, constantly providing them with guidance and leadership while he and they are nurtured by his wife, Tracy.

He is also an inspiration to the Lee & Associates organization with his constant search to self-actualize in so doing becomes a role model for us all. His value to our organization cannot be computed. He uses the Lee & Associates platform to facilitate his localized business plan of office building sales and leases in the Phoenix marketplace.

SECTION I:
DISCOVER EXCELLENCE

CHAPTER 1
THE SPEAKER WHO CHANGED MY LIFE

Bill Lee

During the span of my real estate career, I've witnessed a "pecking order" in many offices. Those at the top are the consistent producers and those at the bottom are the new practitioners. Those in the middle are either on their way to the top, comfortable with their performance in the middle, or slowing down. This pecking order is based on measuring one's sales performance against the other salespeople in the office, company, organization, or industry.

My sales results, over my first seventeen years, were measured in this same way, whether by the manager of the office, my peers, or myself. When I finally found the motivation to make a conscious effort to change this "measurement" and become as good as I could be, I felt like an old-time cartoon character with a light bulb above my head. Suddenly, that bulb lit up, and all the pieces in my life came together to finally make sense.

The choice to chase excellence can't be made for you. You have to make it yourself. Furthermore, you have to commit to it with every fiber of your being and in every aspect of your life. But when you make that decision and commitment to chase excellence, your light bulb will pop on and your eyes will open to the better life you, too, could be enjoying.

For some people, that spark can take place in a single moment, an epiphany of sorts. For others, it's like a light on a dimmer switch—it starts very low then gradually brightens with years of dedication and effort, leading up to the brightest realization that they could pursue a better path.

Maybe for you, that light bulb turning on was what prompted you to read this book. Or maybe at the end of this book you'll be motivated to make your decision to pursue excellence. However it happens, be aware of the moment your light goes on, because that's the moment that your life will change.

It took seventeen years in the business, at age forty-seven, for my light to go on. I finally realized that I wasn't getting the best out of me. I was content with my comparison and competition with others and with my ability to live a comfortable lifestyle where I was.

When I had my epiphany, I learned that if I wanted to accomplish to my level of ability, if I wanted to achieve an improved level of productivity and be the best I could be, I had to commit completely to the path. And it wasn't a one-time idea or a fleeting desire. This would be a daily promise to myself that I would achieve more, win more, and be more.

My moment arrived when I met and listened to a man named Mike Vance at a SIOR (Society of Industrial & Office Brokers) conference. Mike's claim to fame was working with Walt Disney and providing assistance to plan out the specifics of Disneyland. From there, he struck out on his own and started a business helping companies and people organize thought. He would go into a company and teach the people methods to structure their thoughts and ideas. Equally important, he taught people how to follow through by organizing their goals into actionable steps.

As I listened to him speak, I was fascinated by the idea of strategic thought. Organization is a concept that never came easily to me because I stopped at just naming the topics to be organized as opposed to creating

CHAPTER 2

SLOW BUILD

R. Craig Coppola

For Bill, the realization that he wanted to chase excellence in his career and his life, that he wanted to be the best he could be, occurred at a specific moment. He describes it as a light bulb going on suddenly, signaling a change in his thoughts and attitude. Maybe you, too, will experience such an epiphany. The light bulb will go on for you, and you will start down a path toward excellence.

For me, however, the path began as a slow build over time. It started with a desire to win and progressed to a continuous journey toward excellence that I'm still on today.

In this book, Bill and I both talk a lot about sports. As former athletes, we see numerous instances where the lessons learned in athletics can be applied to business. Bill comes from a basketball background; I grew up in a baseball family.

My father was a high school baseball coach. Baseball was his life, and, therefore, mine and my brothers'. He was recently inducted into the Arizona Baseball Coach's Hall of Fame. In high school, both of my older brothers and I played for my father with the Buena High Colts.

questions about a certain aspect of the industry. As we neared completion, we introduced the project to a chosen few real estate directors as well. We spent six months working on this project, three hours a day (11:00 a.m.–2:00 p.m.) for three days a week until we had the idea fully vetted.

We put together a presentation made of ten, six-sided cubes with one photo representing one aspect of the idea on each face of the cube. We would stack these cubes up on the conference table and bring our prospective clients into meetings to discuss the opportunity at hand. Throughout the conversations, they would often ask about some part of the project, and we would pull out one of the cubes and show them how we'd given thought to that aspect and where it fit in with the rest of the plan. It was a tangible, visual way to present all the information that we had spent months developing.

There's a saying in the business that you want to get to a point in your career when people are talking about you positively when you're not in the room. People were talking about us. Our reputation was growing, and many couldn't wait to enter our story room and hear our presentation. When they walked into the room, they could see the entire thought process, all our hard work laid out on the walls, and they knew we were more knowledgeable about the opportunity at hand than any of our peers. The long-term results of this effort were not only significant, but continue to endure to this day to benefit the Lee organization. Unfortunately, a significant recession hit in late '89 shortly after we started the project and I had to wait almost three years to implement the plan (but that's a story for later in the book).

The most rewarding part of the endeavor for me, however, was that I had discovered a new way to accomplish. When you take something from beginning to end, and overcome obstacles along the way, you gain tremendous confidence that makes you feel like you can do anything that you set your mind to. That was me. Suddenly, going forward, I knew that I had it in me to accomplish whatever I put my mind to. With that knowledge, and the successful completion of this project, I gained the confidence to continue pursuing excellence in other ways.

So what's holding you back from pursuing excellence? Has your light bulb started to glow? Don't ignore it. Instead, find ways to make it burn even brighter.

If the matter at hand was important, the process would take time, and if not, it could be vetted quickly. It was like a million new doors of opportunity had opened for me. Furthermore, I could bring others into my room (brain) and leverage their thoughts about my topic at hand. This allowed me to gain residual support in my efforts from those who helped. Those who participated in the process with me often generated follow-up ideas that helped me along the way.

My first significant resolve utilizing this method of structuring thought occurred not too long after I learned Vance's strategy. In 1988, the first Lee & Associates office in Los Angeles was about to open. While driving the geographic area of influence, I recognized a new trend in the industry; one I could see changing the future landscape of a segment of industrial real estate in the nation, and particularly within the territory of the new Lee & Associates office. I knew I needed to get on top of this trend and be prepared to act on the opportunity as quickly as possible. (I'll go into the specifics of this trend later in the book.)

And to do this project right, this new thought structuring process was perfect. As Craig Coppola would say to me, "It's one thing to have an idea; it's another thing to implement the idea." I had the idea, and now I had the tools and the process to bring it to life.

I teamed up with Howard Mann, a self-employed, accomplished industrial realtor, who was a "thinker," an ingredient I came to realize over my years was in short supply in the Commercial Real Estate brokerage industry. Howard loved the idea of strategic thought and had already learned how to use the storyboard process. He had a large conference room in Los Angeles, with four tack walls and a huge conference table and when I told Howard about this new industry trend he jumped in with both feet to help me develop it. With one trip to a supply store, we stocked up on pins, notecards, paper, and pens to get us started, and went to work on this new concept for industrial real estate.

We started pinning up, and then organizing, all our thoughts: products we were interested in, illustrations, clippings from periodicals, ideas and thoughts we had while at our day jobs. We brought in vendors from all walks of life; developers, contractors, architects, subcontractors, users, truckers, suppliers, analysts, retail people, various government agencies, a variety of vendors, anyone we could think of who might be able to answer the action steps necessary to organize each topic. As someone with ADD, I have a lot of ideas flowing through my mind at any given moment. I'm constantly on the receiving end of getting different tangents of thought, but, by 5 o'clock, many of the ideas are gone and are not recoverable. For the better part of my life, the ideas were there; the follow-through wasn't. I had difficulty pinning down and acting on many of my thoughts.

The concept of thought organization was completely foreign to me, the foundation for an entirely new range of processes. While I had achieved success in business without them, I knew that I could be much more effective if I had the tools to structure my thinking.

Part of the way through Vance's talk, a light went on in my head. For me to reach a higher level of success, for me to achieve to my ability, I had to learn how to organize my thoughts and follow through on them. I had to pin down my ideas, organize them into concrete steps and plans, and commit to seeing them through. I also learned to leverage my thoughts through the input of others, by organizing them in such a way that others could visualize the process and were then led into making contributions to help me achieve the goal. With this ability, I would be able to act on the productive thoughts running through my brain, seek the contributions of others, and set my own path to greater accomplishment.

I hired Mike Vance's company, and they set me up with all their tools and concepts. He taught me the basics of "storyboarding," which included creating a "story room," putting my thoughts up on a wall, and going through the process of organizing them. To Mike, every idea was a great idea. He would have me write down every idea and put it up on the wall to see if it fit into the overall picture. If it did, I would leverage it. If it didn't, I got rid of it.

So I started implementing this process. I began with a general theme or topic that required an action plan. Then I would identify the major issues, sub-issues, and abstract thoughts. Eventually, the sub-issues became major issues, and the abstract thoughts found a home. I wrote everything down and pinned my ideas up where I could see them. Through this process, I could take any concept from A to Z and vet it out. In the past, it had been difficult for me to get through C or D, but with this new way of structuring thought, I learned how to keep my focus and get through the entire process.

When my eldest brother was a junior in high school and I was a freshman, my father sat us down and had the college talk with us. He was very candid. He said, "Your mother and I are school teachers. We cannot support you in college. If you want to go to college, you have to earn some type of athletic or academic scholarship, or you're going to have to work your way through school."

I wasn't the best athlete, but I knew that if I wanted to go to college and not have to work my way through school and take out student loans, I was going to need an athletic scholarship. Though I didn't set it down as a specific goal at the time, I kept it at the forefront of my mind over the next four years.

Throughout high school, I played baseball under my father's coaching. I improved a lot, but not enough to earn a full ride to any of the big universities. So at the end of my senior year, I found myself enrolling in junior college at Yavapai Community College.

I played baseball at Yavapai for two years and earned my associate's degree. I was then fortunate to be offered a scholarship to play for a Division I school in Louisiana named Nicholls State University. I played there for my final two years, working my butt off in order to keep my scholarship and improve. My goal evolved from just getting into college playing baseball to getting drafted by a professional team after college. I wasn't ready for my baseball career to end with graduation.

The best players my age started getting drafted their junior year, but it wasn't until the end of my senior year that my ticket came through and I was drafted by the Minnesota Twins organization.

When I was drafted, I had my excellence epiphany. I realized that long-term goals can pay off. If you set your mind to it and work hard, you can achieve anything. Starting my freshman year of high school, my goal of getting a scholarship to play baseball and then be drafted after college occupied my life, and it took eight years for me to get there. But what made this entire journey so unique was that these goals, and the effort to achieve them, weren't a small, one-time desire. It may have started as a goal with a specific end in mind, but it became a long-term mindset. It became who I was, and who I am today.

This pursuit was an eight-year slow build that changed my whole perspective on just about everything. For starters, I had put my mind, heart, and effort toward something, and I got it. That proved to me that, going forward, I knew I could bet on myself. I knew if I wanted something, I would have enough confidence in myself to do the hard work and win. That is incredibly empowering when you think about it. And I believe anyone can attain this learned behavior and mindset.

I adopted a long-term focus with the belief that anything was possible. So when I entered the business world a year later, I took that mindset with me. Unlike Bill, who came to this realization several years into his career, I began my career with the intention to win every single day. I knew I could because I had already done it. I just had to focus on the hard work of learning the game. That took a lot of time and effort, which experience had demonstrated would pay off in the long run.

Today I can look back and say with certainty that my epiphany came from my baseball background. It taught me discipline, how to take direction from a coach, and how to put in long hours of work. I had experienced the process of setting a long-term goal and chasing it relentlessly, and I had tasted sweet victory when it came to fruition. When I went into the business world, all I had to do was transfer that mindset and those behaviors to a new area of my life. And I haven't stopped.

Living a life chasing excellence is taking that mindset of setting long-term goals and committing to them with discipline and applying it to every part of your life. When you consistently achieve those wins, your confidence grows, and you want to set and achieve more goals. At least that's how I've evolved. It's a constant process, a way of life. And it's 100 percent possible for you, too, as long as you set a goal and pursue it relentlessly through hard work every single day. You will win, and with each accomplishment you'll build confidence in yourself, which prepares you for your next pursuit. That's living a life chasing excellence.

CHAPTER 3

HIGHWAYS OF LIFE: BLACK, WHITE, & GRAY

Bill Lee

When setting out to write this book, I had no idea what it would become. I thought I might record some of my ideas and experiences in the Commercial Real Estate business and share them with other brokers in the Lee & Associates organization. I never considered attempting to write a book to share with people outside the company until Craig Coppola and I discussed the idea.

Even as we started meeting and collecting stories, I still never intended to create a how-to-be-successful book. That's not what I wanted, nor did I believe I had enough expertise to coach people on excellence. It is such a unique thing, this journey to excellence; no two journeys look the same, and the results certainly vary from person to person. So how could I attempt to teach others how to chase their own perception of excellence?

But as I began writing, I kept in mind my belief about the three highways to pursue productivity, a concept I'll share with you.

I believe that there are three highways in life, especially in commercial real estate, that we use to transport our efforts to accomplish goals. The black highway is a route that tells us what we should not do. The white highway is a route that tells us what we should do. And the gray highway is an uncharted route that we travel with experience and thought that allows for bold, new, and undiscovered avenues for accomplishment.

As brokers, we can live in all three. Our business is truly unique because it, more than almost any other industry, is one that we get to build for ourselves. There are fundamentals to learn (which we will discuss later), but for the most part, the job is what you make of it. You learn and understand; the basics, the market, strategies, prospecting, relationships, transaction opportunities, negotiations, fee sharing, and platforms. This process happens every single day, but I guarantee you that when you compare two brokers, their manner and methods are usually very different.

In my career, I have met and worked alongside hundreds upon hundreds of brokers, and many have their own style of securing business. Their systems and mannerisms and basic beliefs typically can be very different. In writing this book, I met with and interviewed several very accomplished peers, and each placed emphasis on different parts of the business that were the most important to them. And yet, despite the fact that they all were so different, I can still group them together as great brokers, excellent in their pursuit of success. They all have something in them that makes them stand out.

That's why I want to start off this book with a discussion of this highway of gray and a disclaimer. The advice in the pages to come follows that highway of gray. It is not my intention for you to do things exactly the way I did; or the way my colleague, Craig Coppola did; or anyone else that we discuss in the book. The journey to excellence rides the highway of gray, a highway of beliefs and methods that deliver success for some and not for others. It's up to you to decide which ones are best for you, and what you can create for yourself from this inspiration as you recognize that the commercial real estate industry is constantly in a state of change and that these changes can be incremental or fundamental.

The point of this book is to present stories of people who have chased excellence and achieved a high level of success. The hope is that you will glean some inspiration from their stories and be motivated to grow and improve in your own life, chasing the best version of yourself. The advice we share we've recorded because we truly believe it can help you on your journey. But only you can decide what's best for you.

That being said, you shouldn't go into this book with a black or white highway mindset.

It won't benefit you to take the white highway and apply every single piece of advice in the exact manner that Craig and I did. Your life, circumstances, passions, market, etc. are very unique, and the odds are, if you tried to copy us exactly you would not find your true excellence.

Let it also be understood that the business of commercial real estate can change daily with new thoughts, ideas, technology, support, as well as changing market, business, and construction trends. You can become old news overnight if you are not continually on the lookout for these changing dynamics in the industry.

You should also not approach this book on the black highway, ignoring the advice, or reading it and thinking that you could never do something similar. Go into each chapter and read our stories with an open mind. If you read something and think, "I can't do that," well, then, guess what? You're right—you won't do it. I believe that whoever you are, you can do whatever you set your mind to, and it may be just a matter of understanding of where your greatest joy will come from. I can assure you, though, that you will not be able to make that assessment accurately until you commit to the effort of self-actualizing.

Take the highway of gray. It's not a bad place to be. It opens you up to many possibilities and allows you to make your own choices. Too many people live on the black or white highway. They stay cut off from possibility, looking at new opportunities with a closed mind, and never move beyond their small comfort zone. Or they become "yes men and women," doing what they are told to do without thinking about the particular relevance who they are and their own special brand of uniqueness. Then, they either overwhelm themselves or fail at something they should have known was not in their best interest.

Stack your capabilities, preferences, and circumstances against our stories and suggestions, and learn how you can embark on your own excellence journey.

CHAPTER 4

THE PHOTOCOPIER SALESMAN

Bill Lee

Before I got into the business of commercial real estate, I sold office products, primarily photocopiers, for a living. I worked for 3M, a company that had a great training program with competent sales managers who were groomed for the job from successful personal sales experience. It was my first sales job, and all we did all day, every day, was make cold calls to gain product presentations and then "ask for the order."

The product wasn't the best product on the market. But this was not necessarily a bad thing for my sales training. It meant that I had to sell harder and faster. I had to cover more territory and beat the Xerox guy to the next office.

My whole pitch revolved around features, advantages, and benefits of the various office products that I sold. We were measured by how many cold calls, demonstrations, and sales we made per week. This was a perfect job for me in this stage of my business career because I was competitive and was always striving to increase my numbers and was held accountable for the results. I stayed three years, and even today I can't believe I stayed that long since other, higher-paying sales opportunities were available.

The biggest problem with selling 3M's top machine, the 209, was that it wasn't just our best model; it was also our biggest. It was huge—maybe six feet in length and weighing more than one hundred pounds.

I worked in West L.A., which wasn't a bad territory, but it did have a lot of two-story walk-up office buildings with no elevators. I often had to carry this big machine up a couple flights of stairs to make my pitch to the tenants of these second-story offices. That was not easy to do.

One sales presentation I remember vividly. The company was located on one of those two-story walk-ups, so I carefully lugged my machine up the stairs and made a demonstration of the 209. It was a hot September day, with the temperature in the upper 90s. That heat stays with you all day, no matter how long you spend in an air-conditioned office.

I gave a good demonstration of the machine to a group of guys in the office and used a site seller, a stand-up binder that showed the quality of all the different kinds of copies you could make with this machine. I put the site seller down on the table for them to look at, and made my presentation. Unfortunately, I couldn't close the sale. They were nice enough, but after I was done I had to pack up my machine, and carry it all the way back down the stairs and to my company car that allowed for the collapsible stand to be pushed into the rear of the vehicle.

When I reached my car, I realized that I had left my site seller back in the office. So I went back upstairs and opened the door, just in time to hear them talking about me. "How'd you like to be that sorry S.O.B. and sell that machine at this time of the day?" one guy was saying. It was the first time I realized that maybe there might be something else out there in the business world for me besides selling copiers.

Not long after, I was at a wedding as a member of the wedding party, and another person in the wedding party explained to me that he was making three times what I was selling commercial real estate. I looked him over and quickly figured that he wasn't three times better than me. So off I went to quit my job at 3M and take my wife, child, and baby in the hopper, house payment, car payment, and three months' savings, to pursue a new career selling commercial real estate with Grubb & Ellis with no salary. Not the best of circumstances for a young married man with a family, but again sometimes the harder it is the better it is. When your back is to the wall, you become more courageous and your sense of priority becomes more acute. I needed to make money, so making calls and asking for the order took precedent over everything else.

Even in commercial real estate, though, the path to excellence is paved with thankless jobs. But it's in these positions that you often learn some of the most important lessons that guide you to your calling and purpose. Lugging that copier across Los Angeles was a brutal job, but it gave me the necessary sales skills and competitive drive that stayed with me throughout my brokerage career. I can name several other tasks I performed as a broker that seemed tedious at the time but provided experience that later became extremely useful.

None, however, were more important than prospecting and generating opportunities to pay the bills and to utilize the efforts already made in preparation for these opportunities. Prioritizing the value of the many work tasks is essential for success. I've seen many capable people fail because they did what they enjoyed doing rather than what *needed* to be done for success first.

Now, let's come to an understanding about the commercial real estate business. Just like selling photocopiers wasn't a level playing field—Xerox had the best machines in the late 60's and all the others fell in line behind their product—neither is selling commercial real estate. Engaging in a relationship with either an owner or a tenant most times puts you second to an agent who already knows those parties. Only after previous successful interactions with these people will you have an advantage or, at the least, a level playing field.

So it is incumbent on you to win the business. You need to be better. You need to understand the need, the market and be able to succinctly explain your expertise, capability, and value to the client. This process takes thought, which at times seems tedious, but is always necessary. Too many times this process becomes routine without thought. Would you play a competitive game without practicing? Would you give a performance without practicing? Would you make a meaningful speech without preparing? Why then would you see a client unprepared? Why then does it happen day in and day out?

Don't freeze in the face of this kind of work. Don't write it off as unimportant. And especially don't undervalue the lessons it teaches you.

CHAPTER 5
COMMIT OR EXIST
Bill Lee

Why is the concept of commitment so hard for people these days? It seems everywhere you look people have trouble committing: faith, jobs, diets, workouts, marriages, etc. The sad truth is the number of people who quit exceeds the number of people who stick with it and make it happen by a large multiplier.

Part of the problem is, we live in a society that is constantly updating itself with the "newer and better." This fear of commitment stops many people from ever starting. How sad is that?

Commitment is the foundation for every endeavor. Everything from getting out of bed in the morning to achieving your dreams starts with a commitment. You will never succeed at anything if you don't get comfortable with the idea of committing. That's just the way life is.

My early commitments were selling raffle tickets in grammar school, showing up and folding newspapers on time for my paper route, attending practice every day for high school sports, coaching youth sports for my kids, buying my first house, making cold calls at 3M, entering the commercial real estate industry with no salary, and leaving my job at Grubb & Ellis to start Lee & Associates. But chasing excellence—that is taking commitment to a new level. That takes an almost hourly planned and prepared commitment. It's a commitment to yourself that you will become excellent.

In the course of writing this book, I've had an opportunity to interview several successful salespeople and peers in the industry. My mission was to get their take on excellence and how they achieved it. I hand-selected these people not only because of their accomplishments professionally, but how they live their lives in general.

Jeff Smith is a walking case study for excellence. He currently works in the Lee & Associates Ontario office in California. He is more than just a business associate; our friendship goes way back to when he attended high school with two of my sons.

Scoring well on tests came easily to Jeff in school, so he skated through high school and college without real commitment. Athletically, he was gifted, if you could call a 44-inch vertical jump and 4.4 on the forty-yard dash being gifted. He excelled in volleyball, football, and basketball, and participated in both high school and college sports, but I'm sure he would say that he never came close to accomplishing at the level of his ability. Of course, most athletes will tell you that they were never as good as they could have been, while also never as good as they thought they were at the time.

In school, Jeff admits, he could do minimal work and do well enough to get by. Even though his grades were good, he wasn't dedicated to his studies. Furthermore, he wasn't dedicated to learning; he was just existing. But Jeff was smart, charming, and good with people, so when he came looking for a job, I hired him.

I immediately assigned him to my Just-in-Time delivery concept, which involved build-to-suit warehouse transactions that were satisfying a new and growing industry need, a concept I alluded to in an earlier chapter. By the time Jeff joined our team, this approach had taken off and it was a huge portion of our Los Angeles business.

Jeff did a good job on that project, but in a moment of truth he told me that he couldn't wait to go home every day and drink beer and surf. He just wasn't as motivated or committed as I'd hoped he would be. He maintained the 9-to-5 workday mentality, getting through his work quickly so he could go home and enjoy his evenings off. Still, he performed well and did good work for us, so, just as he had in school, he skated by in business for a few years. Again, he was existing, but nothing more.

One day, out of the blue, he came into my office and asked if he could transition to a growth office in Ontario. I could tell, suddenly, there was a new fire in his eyes. He was excited about the industrial work the Ontario office was doing, and wanted to put his attention there. At the time, I didn't understand the sudden change, but I went with my gut and his fire, signed off on his transfer, and wished him luck.

I later discovered that he requested this change around the same time he met his future wife. As their relationship grew more serious, he realized that he, too, needed to become more serious. Years later, when he told me this story, he put it into interesting words. He said, "I finally decided to commit to commit."

Here was a guy who had never committed to anything. He had never needed to, and his life had been working just fine. But then, he decided to commit to becoming a person who commits. I had never thought of commitment in that context before. Commit to commit. Three simple words, with huge implications. It made me realize that you don't have to find something to commit to before you become a committed person. Often by being that person, the thing worth committing to finds you.

We all begin, but many times when we begin something new, we don't know how to really jump in and get started. We just do tasks and exist. We may have a little direction, but most of the time, whatever the endeavor, we really don't think through our path. Maybe we put our plan together the night before, if that. That behavior is a symptom of a lack of commitment and it's a red flag for just existing. And once in that pattern, it's hard to become committed. Who wants to be committed to that feeling of "spinning your wheels"? It's not even in the realm of our consciousness. So we continue to exist.

Jeff's comment made me think about how much time I had wasted simply existing when I first got started in this business; how many times I started, failed, and started again without any careful planning or real commitment. The short answer is, a lot. There were times when I thought I'd made a commitment to my career and to being the best, but really all

I'd done was make a commitment to showing up to the office, being competitive, and going through the motions; existing a little better than I had in the past. When something didn't work, I'd chalk it up to any of a variety of external forces. I didn't believe my inability to commit had anything to do with it; the problem was always someone or something else. But the real problem was that I didn't commit to committing to be excellent.

It took me a long time to realize that real commitment is not just a commitment to doing something. It's a commitment to doing something the right way. Jeff had committed to working for me, and he did a good job. But he was the first one out of the office every night. He never had a real dedication to the job until he found someone who motivated him to make a more serious commitment to committing, to move beyond existing.

If you have trouble understanding this idea of "commit to commit," think of your favorite athlete or athletes in general. Athletics is a wonderful endeavor because it teaches us all how to commit. You don't get much playing time if you just exist on a team. We measure athletes by the success they have and the level of commitment they make. This is especially relevant for athletes who might not have the inherent talent to compete at their desired level.

There are hundreds of stories of frustrated athletes who underachieved, never making it as far as they could have for a variety of reasons that kept them from a fulfilling experience in the sport of their choice. And there is the opposite, the best and most widely known examples of which are Bill Russell and Michael Jordan, both cut from their freshman basketball teams. Can you imagine if they had quit then and there, deciding that the commitment wasn't worth it?

In our life as commercial realtors, we do not have the same physical limitations that athletes face. We need few natural abilities to take us to the heights of the business. But what we do need is a desire to move beyond existing and fully commit. The most inspiring news of all is that we can foster a commitment to excel and realize it. It just takes, as Jeff put it so well, a commitment to commit.

To me, this is the most powerful commitment of all, because once you make it, you find nothing holding you back from reaching your goal or that next level. Your achievement of just about anything becomes that much easier because you know that nothing except your own insecurities can hold you back.

When you look at commitment in that way, it's a no brainer! You become much stronger in your actions and in your convictions. That commitment not only pushes you to perform at a higher level, it also earns you respect from the people around you. Think about it. Who would you rather do a deal with: someone known for saying yes and being average, or someone who always follows through on his, or her promises, and chases excellence? Being able to commit—committing to commit—is often a key indicator of how successful you will be.

Like most things we will discuss in this book, committing is not easy. Commitment requires mental strength, discipline, and conscious thought. It also requires balance. But if you can move beyond just existing and commit to commit to excellence, you will encounter great success on that path.

CHAPTER 6

NOTHING IN MODERATION

R. Craig Coppola

In my mind, the journey to excellence can be summed up in a single phrase: nothing in moderation. Much like Jeff Smith's commitment to commit, nothing in moderation is an all-or-nothing kind of lifestyle.

Kathy Heasley and I came up with this phrase when we were writing my first book, *How to Win in Commercial Real Estate Investing*. I was trying to summarize the underlying theme of my life. I looked at my achievements, my goals, my career, and my life, and decided that the reason I had been so successful in these areas was that I didn't do anything in moderation. I gave in excess to each endeavor. I didn't hold anything back. When I wanted something, I went for it with every last bit of energy and focus I had.

I think this "rule" also encapsulates chasing excellence in commercial real estate because, in that journey, you have to give everything you have in order to set yourself apart. Moderation produces mediocrity. There is no place for mediocrity on the road to excellence. If you want to be excellent, you have to give that extra bit to rise above the crowd. The only way you can do that is by holding nothing back.

As Oscar Wilde said, "Nothing succeeds like excess." The only way you will achieve your goals is by throwing doubt into the wind and pursuing your dreams, whole-heartedly.

Cultivating this "nothing in moderation" mindset is not for the faint of heart. The idea behind it is draining. It squeezes every last bit of energy and focus from you. It demands your time, your passion, your confidence; everything. You can't dip a toe into the pool of excellence; you need to swan dive in.

All of this comes with a huge caveat: "nothing in moderation" forces you to prioritize. It demands clarity, and it only works with alignment to the rest of your life. Like everything in life, you have to have boundaries and restrictions. Of course, there are things that you know you can't give up to chase excellence in your career, such as family time. So the key to nothing in moderation becomes clarity—in your goals, in your purpose, and in your priorities.

Before you chase after your dreams, it becomes mandatory that you know precisely what your goals are, and your purpose or reason for pursuing them. Before you can commit, before you can go full force on anything, you have to know exactly what you want and why. If you can articulate those reasons, write them down and hang them above your desk, it becomes easier to let go of your fears and doubts to give your all to this endeavor.

You also need clarity in your priorities. This includes ranking the things that are the most important to you, and itemizing those things you cannot give up in this pursuit. If you are totally committed, that list should be relatively short. "Nothing in moderation" means making sacrifices to achieve your goals.

When you combine this clarity with your passion and determination, it will be impossible for you to be average.

When we started Lee & Associates Arizona, I had absolute clarity of goals and purpose. I knew I wanted to be the best broker in the market. I had purpose and drive. I wanted to be recognized as the best. This manifested itself in being the Top Producing Broker for the Year. I've achieved that goal almost every year for the past twenty-five years. I know without any uncertainty, going into each year, that I want to be that man.

After many years on the board of the Arizona chapter of NAIOP, I worked my way up to serve as the NAIOP president. I wanted to give back to the industry that helped my career. When I took the position on, I committed myself to it completely. It became a number one focus, and I devoted hours of time going above and beyond the average presidential duties. That year, I won Chapter President of the Year for NAIOP National. I wasn't content to skate by, to get the job done and do nothing more. When I make a commitment and put my mind to something, I intend to be the best. And the only way to achieve that kind of excellence is by doing nothing in moderation.

If something is important enough to you that you commit your time and energy to it, why would you half-ass it? Why wouldn't you go full force into your pursuit, setting your sights on the highest bar? I will never understand the kind of people who are content to coast by and remain average. If you're reading this book, chances are you are not one of those people. You desire something more out of your life: excellence. This is one way to get it.

PLATFORM PROFILE
Darla Longo (CBRE GROUP, INC.)

I've known Darla for her entire career and she has continually pushed the envelope, even re-inventing herself at times. She has certainly brought her own brand of excellence along with her to new and higher levels of sales, to where she currently resides. She has created a platform involving Coldwell Banker Richard Ellis's (CBRE) best and brightest national institutional investment sales team. Darla has always been the ultimate team player, bringing others with her along the way to creative new platforms at CBRE.

I had the following conversation with her recently in which she said "I love the business and strive for growth and excellence. When I struggle, or lose, I use that as an opportunity to retool and grow. Relationships are very important to me. I really care about always doing 'the next right thing.' The more I give the more I get back. I do strive to be one of the best of the best in the business and that is what motivates me." My sense is that Darla sees the transaction as a step in the relationship and is not driven, as others might be, to place undue importance on the amount of the fee when compared to the importance of the long-term relationship.

Her instincts have provided special and necessary insights to the CBRE Board for more than a decade. She is ageless, another fierce competitor still going strong who still finds time to be a spouse, mother, and sibling to her large, extended family. Her level of sales success has endured over thirty years and she has always achieved at unprecedented levels. She maintains relationships that have lasted several decades and always finds time to add more to the list.

Now at a level where she is viewed as an expert and consultant in commercial property institutional sales, her guidance and assistance are often sought out by the "who's who" in the commercial real estate industry. The platform that CBRE provides Darla is that of the largest commercial real estate organization in the world; a firm of unprecedented resources, locations and support made available to its employees. No matter the market, you can be guaranteed that CBRE will be one your major competitors. I have great respect for this firm and its employees. And above all, I have great respect and admiration for Darla.

SECTION II:
PREPARE FOR EXCELLENCE

CHAPTER 7

EXCELLENCE AND THE JUMP SHOT

Bill Lee

So you think you're ready to take the big step, to commit to excellence, embrace a nothing-in-moderation-mindset, and start going after those life-changing transactions? Wait just one minute.

Rome wasn't built in a day, and neither were the careers of the most successful business men and women. Rather than leaping at those big deals right away, let's put on the brakes and go back to the beginning for a second. Let's focus on some fundamentals.

Master the fundamentals and you'll gain a solid foundation upon which to build your career. Understanding the basics is what will allow you to recognize changes and shifts in the market, how they impact the business today, and what the impact will be in the future. The fundamentals will also be the things that catch you when you fall, and if you are like most professionals in this business, you will fall often.

Maybe it's because I am a sports guy, but I see the commercial real estate business like I see sports: the thrill of competition, the high highs and the low lows, the importance of fundamentals and practice, and the ability to execute when the game is on the line. After playing basketball competitively, and teaching and coaching at the high school level immediately after college, I continued the coaching pursuit as a volunteer with my own sons. When they reached the high school level, I continued to coach seventh and eighth grade boys at the schools that my own sons had attended.

Boys at that age are fun to be around, as they are eager to learn and still carry the dream of becoming an NBA player. It's also the age when they begin to learn the jump shot. I bring it up now as an illustration of learning the basics of CRE and business life in general. Keep it simple, prioritize, do it, put in the time, and you will gain a competitive advantage.

After so many years of coaching basketball, I had refined my teaching method to the point where I could teach any thirteen-year-old boy how to shoot a jump shot in ten minutes. Basketball is all about fundamentals, so the carrot of learning this shot became a great bargaining tool for the kids on the team who gave me difficulty. "Get with the program and I'll teach you how to shoot a jump shot." It worked just about every time.

Teaching the jump shot is easy if you take it in a sequence. Try it with your child, niece or nephew, or grandchild. Go through the list step by step, practicing each step a few times until mastered before moving on to the next.

1. Have the person you are teaching jump up in the air. Okay, so now you know the athlete can jump.

2. Ask the shooter to lie on his or her back on the ground with a smaller ball, like a handball, and release the ball correctly above his or her head a few feet in the air.

3. Have the shooter stand up, take an imaginary ball and move it above his or her head while standing still, just like with the handball.

4. Now, have your student do the same thing while jumping and shoot the shot without a ball, making sure that the shot comes at the top of the jump and not on the way up.

5. Next, do the same thing with the handball and have the shooter shoot to you while standing a few feet away from you. Catch it by holding your hands above your head.

6. Now do the same thing with the shooter simply shooting the handball toward the basket, rather than trying to make the shot.

7. Refine the shot with a lighter, smaller handball—on a smaller rim if necessary—until your shooter is ready to try it with a basketball.

The strong kids can do steps one through seven in a single ten-minute session, while the smaller, weaker kids will take longer. But what a joy to see them make their first "jumper"—and you'd better believe they will continue to practice that shot from then on.

Although this is a how-to guide you can try yourself or share with family members who enjoy playing the game, this is also a great metaphor for the discipline required in real estate. Learn to shoot the jump shot. It's a progression of steps until you reach the final goal. That's how I taught new salespeople: a sequence of smaller tasks that lead to larger accomplishments. I didn't start them out closing deals or even meeting with clients until I was sure they had mastered the fundamentals which would allow them greater understanding while attending meetings and, in time, allow them to even bring value to the meetings.

And of course, you don't shoot a perfect jump shot or win in commercial real estate by doing these six steps just once. You have to practice the process over and over again.

The point is you have to begin somewhere. Even with all the energy you are feeling right now to dive in and start chasing excellence now, you can't expect to go out and land a huge deal on your first day in the office, or your second day, or your third. The disappointment of failing to achieve those big deals right off the bat is what causes all too many people with excellent potential to give up. Understanding that you have to start with the commitment to your goal of excellence, then the commitment to learn the fundamentals, building on them until you reach your goal, is what separates the wishful from the successful.

So what are the fundamentals of commercial real estate you have to master first?

1. **Know the market.** The best way to let people know you exist is to be of value to them. The only way you can be of value is if you know something about the market that they don't know. You have to do your homework and in truth there's no shortcut for driving your market; learning the tenant base, the ownership base, rents and values, vacancy, trends past and present, and future projections; and then building a relationship with all impacting vendors.

2. **Master prospecting.** There are a myriad of ways to prospect today but to be engaging and filled with specific knowledge is essential for a maximum result. Regardless of the tools, your success resides in letting people know that you exist with a cornucopia of resources at your disposal. How do you communicate to these prospects? Make sure you give your dialogue thought. Remember, you only have a quick minute or two to allow your prospect to think about your value points. Introduce them within the first minute of dialogue.

3. **Learn the process.** The best basketball players know the process for making the shots that score points. They know them so well that they become reflexes. They see the patterns and can respond without thinking. That needs to be you in the game of commercial real estate.

4. **Develop relationships.** In the process, when you do the previous three things, you can't help but build relationships. And it's the relationships you make that help you to become excellent.

Benchmarking yourself against these basics and tracking your progress is what will allow you to see the changes occurring within yourself and the market. It will show you what you need to do to take yourself further and further, until you are sinking your commercial real estate jump shot every single time.

CHAPTER 8

SETTING MYSELF UP FOR SUCCESS

R. Craig Coppola

The fundamentals make up the foundation of every endeavor you take on. Mastering them is part of your preparation for excellence, laying the groundwork to build on your achievements to reach greater wins. But before you begin practicing these fundamentals, you'll need a little foresight and preparation to ensure that you not only learn them, but make them stick.

When I make a commitment to do something, I put everything I have into it (nothing in moderation again). So when I stopped playing baseball after being released from the Minnesota Twins organization, and made the transition to real estate, I devoted almost all of my time to it. Okay, I devoted *all* my time to it.

After about seven years, I started to feel the burn-out. I was devoting way too much time to work, and I was starting to miss being active and competing athletically. I found myself searching for something to fill the athletic gap that had been left when I left baseball.

Martial arts was something I had always been drawn to, so I thought, "Now is the time." I dove in, immediately setting my first goal for myself to earn a black belt. For me, success in martial arts would be attaining that status. But it wouldn't be as simple as signing up for any old class.

Like Bill says, fundamentals are everything. In this case, the fundamentals included doing my homework and learning all I could. So I began researching different types of martial arts: Karate, Tae Kwon Do, Kung Fu, Jujitsu, etc. I wanted to know what they were about, what made them different, and which style appealed to me the most.

Then I looked within a three-mile radius of my house, and interviewed four different dojos. I knew a fundamental of my success would be to limit my travel time; I needed to find a place close by. Only then would I be able to truly commit to reaching my goal. Eventually, I settled on a Tae Kwon Do studio close to my house, with great instructors. I believed in the message of this type of martial arts, and the dojo had everything I needed to be successful.

For the next three years, I disciplined myself to learn Tae Kwon Do. There were some group classes, but the majority of my training was through private lessons. Because of my time schedule, I needed to train early in the morning, and no one was doing classes at 5:00 a.m. I knew if I just went to classes at the normal time, I would not be able to commit to them as much. It would only work for me if I trained early.

My instructor's name was David Karstadt. He was a father of four, the owner of the studio, and, after much cajoling on my part, the only instructor willing to get up at 5:00 a.m. For three years we beat the sun. He got up and trained me. He was as disciplined as I was, and I earned my black belt. I had achieved my goal.

But as you'll discover, when you chase excellence it's never about achieving your goal. It's always about the pursuit, the journey toward your goal. You set yourself up for success, and once you achieve that goal, you move on to a new one.

My new goal became to get my second degree black belt (in Tae Kwon Do there are nine degrees of black belts). Fewer than 10 percent of people who start martial arts get a black belt, but fewer than 2 percent get a second degree black belt, and I wanted to push myself to be in that smaller percentile.

So I decided to go after it. At this point, David Karstadt was fading on morning training; he wasn't willing to get up early with me early anymore. He turned me over to his son John, who was twenty years younger than me but a complete martial arts superstar. John trained me for two more years until I got my second degree belt.

After taking a year off, you guessed it, I went back to the dojo and started training for my third degree belt. It took me four more years with John to achieve that next level, and by then I was in my early forties, well into my brokerage career. When I achieved my third degree designation, it was time for me to be done.

Those years I spent training for my black belts taught me a lot about discipline, hard work, competition, and more. But the main reason I was able to achieve my three goals was, I had set myself up for success from the very start.

When I embarked on the road of martial arts, I had my definition of success in mind: get a black belt. Most people, when they set a goal like that, believe that the journey is simple. You want a black belt, so you sign up for classes and train until you get it. They don't take the time to properly set themselves up for success. They pick a studio nearby, they start taking classes, and when it doesn't work out they blame other factors—like a busy schedule, the instructor, you name it—for their failure.

If you really want to be successful and achieve your goal, you're going to have to put in a lot more work than just showing up and going through the motions. Everyone performs at his or her best under different circumstances. But in order to be successful, you have to truly know yourself and know the kind of environment and structure you need to thrive. Only once you've taken the time to set up that kind of environment can you be successful.

Another example of trying to set myself up for success is dieting. Over the years, I've tried almost every diet there is, hoping to lose weight. The problem is; I have a massive sweet tooth. I've tried diets that mix exercise and healthier eating, but still allow me my sweets and my carbs. I always wonder at the end of these diets why I haven't lost any weight or seen the results I want.

Eventually, I discovered that in order for me to be successful in my diets, I have to cut out all the good stuff. I can't let myself cheat at all, because I have no self-control. Once I've taken a bite of that brownie, I know I'm going to have at least three more.

My wife is different. When she goes on a diet, she can contain herself. She can limit herself to one piece of chocolate after a day of healthy eating, and not fall any further off the wagon. I wish I had that restraint.

Once I recognized what I needed to be successful in my eating habits, I made sure to set myself up for success every time I started a new diet. I got rid of all the sweets in the house and I cut out the carbs completely. I won't even let myself have a taste because I know myself well enough to know what would happen next. And you know what? I've seen great results.

If you want something, you have to take the time to understand what will make you successful in your pursuit. You have to do your homework, learn the fundamentals, and set a structure in place that allows you to perform at your best. No matter if it's a business or personal goal, take the time to outline what you need to be successful. Don't skimp on the planning process, either. Don't be afraid to ask your gym instructor to meet you earlier if you get your best workouts done in the morning. Don't settle for a desk right in the middle of the hectic office if you need peace and quiet to complete your best work. Once you start compromising, you start lessening your chances of success.

When you understand the things you need to be successful in your life, you will be so much closer to paving the way to excellence.

CHAPTER 9

PUT YOURSELF IN THE RIGHT ENVIRONMENT

Bill Lee

Speaking of setting yourself up for success, there's one big external factor you need to give some consideration before you dive into this journey. Sure, a big part of success is certainly based on your internal drive and your commitment to being the best you can be. But there is a part of excellence that can boost your performance that lies outside your control. The market direction, the actions of others, health concerns, government policies, your work "platform"—all of these and more can affect your personal path to excellence. You have to learn to work with both types of factors in order to increase your own success.

So let's forget about the external factors you can't control and talk about a big one you can: your workplace environment. It is up to you to define and create it. Maybe you like more solitude, a quite workspace away from the chaos of a large, corporate office. Or maybe you need organized chaos, with lots of people running around, sharing ideas and information, and providing motivation. Whatever that environment looks like for you, you have to take the time to cultivate it either by yourself or with your team members, addressing all important needs, so that it provides you and your fellow associates the tools for personal success.

Tim Cronin was running into a stone wall in the early years of his career. He was not achieving his desired level of success in our Irvine office. He was working a market outside of Irvine that he couldn't physically get to because of traffic. He also worked with people who didn't work that market, so he couldn't share his information, needs, contacts, etc., with others; couldn't learn from them; and couldn't bounce ideas off of them. In addition, the manager of the office wasn't able to support Tim because the manager came from a background in the retail specialty, and Tim was working in industrial. The manager didn't understand the industrial market that Tim was working in and could not effectively guide him.

Tim wasn't in an environment that provided him a foundation for success. It wasn't until he moved offices and put himself in the right environment, surrounded by the proper support team of other industrial brokers, that he was able to flourish. Now, he's been in the top-producing echelon of brokers in the new office for the past twenty-five years. Changing the environment and team changed his entire career.

Do you feel like you aren't thriving? Or that your environment is holding you back? Maybe it's because it isn't the right environment for you to succeed. Identify areas where you aren't getting the support that you need to win. This might mean switching offices, teams, specialties, or even careers. Change can be scary, but sometimes that switch is exactly what you need to jump-start your efforts toward excellence.

CHAPTER 10

IT ALL COMES BACK TO CHON-JI

R. Craig Coppola

Not long after I attained my third degree black belt and decided to end my training in Tae Kwon Do, my instructor, David Karstadt, got a call from the USA International Tae Kwon Do Federation. The world championship in Tae Kwon Do was coming up the next year, and the U.S. had never had a team win a medal. In the past, the U.S. had had several individuals win medals, but had never won an overall team medal.

The reason for this, the Federation believed, was that the U.S. team always took the top six individuals in the country to compete. They asked these solo stars to become a team practically overnight, which wasn't going to happen. They were from all over the country, had never trained together, and were very devoted to their individual success. There could be no hope of winning a team medal with this process.

That year, the championship was returning to its roots, to its birth country of South Korea. General Choi, the founder of Tae Kwon Do, had recently passed away, so for the first time ever, the championship was being held in his homeland. This was a very special competition, and the USA Federation wanted to put together a team that could compete and take home a team medal.

So they decided to do something different. They split the country into four different regions, called a coach in each region, and asked them to put together a team to represent their region in a national competition. The winning team would represent the USA at the world championship.

David Karstadt was asked to coach the Southwest team. David put together a team that included his two sons, John and Joe; and three other superstars from Texas, New Mexico, and Arizona. Then he called me.

I was not a superstar in Tae Kwon Do, not by any stretch, but David and John knew that I would show up, be disciplined, and motivate the others to do the same. So the Southwest team consisted of six members: five young superstars and me, the 44-year-old just lucky to be along for the ride.

Given our work schedules, we had to practice early. We trained four days a week at 4:30 in the morning. It was obvious that the other team members were superstars, but some days the superstars didn't show up. Some days they didn't perform their best.

During the entire training process, I became not just the old guy, but the organization and motivation coach. They knew the technique, but I was the one who insisted that we had to do this every day; we had to push through the daily grind to become the best.

Months later, we won the USA championship and became the official USA team. Then we had six months to train for the world championship, and again, during that time, my value had little to do with Tae Kwon Do, but had a lot to do with showing up every day, conquering the grind, and motivating the others to do the same.

There were four events in the Tae Kwon Do competition we had to train for:

1. Specialty breaking—breaking boards using high kicks, jumping kicks, back kicks, and other specialized movements. This was not my event.

2. Power breaking—which includes breaking up to four or five boards at a time with sheer power. This was also not my event.

3. Fighting—full-contact fighting. I participated in this event with four of the other team members.

4. Patterns—choreographed, sequenced movements. There are twelve patterns that everyone in the tournament had to know, and officials would tell you just before you went on which one you would perform. As an individual doing patterns, you just follow the movements, but as a team, there are all kinds of special things you can do. You can have rippling effects with half the team moving one way while the other half moves another, and all manner of other special tricks. This was my comfort zone.

In the last month of training before the competition, we had one pattern left to put our own unique spin on. It was the very first pattern that all beginners in Tae Kwon Do learn, called "Chon-Ji." Few teams ever take the time to personalize Chon-Ji because it's the simplest pattern ever, created by General Choi, with only nineteen movements.

At this point in the training, everyone was burned out, and no one wanted to put in the early mornings or the effort to making this pattern unique. We all knew the movements, and everyone was exhausted. But we made the decision to keep pushing through, and worked on rippling this pattern, making it really cool, and continuing to put in the hard work through that final month of training.

When we arrived at the tournament in South Korea, we had to compete against sixty-five countries, the best in the world. We sailed through the semis and made it to the finals. The competition narrowed down to our USA team and Japan in the finals.

The final event was Patterns. Each team performed two patterns pulled from a hat. At the end of the round, we were tied.

The competition went into overtime, and the two teams went head to head on one last pattern. The pattern they pulled from the hat? You guessed it: Chon-Ji. Immediately, we knew that we had this medal in the bag.

Japan's team performed their version, which was just the entire team doing the motions in sync, and then it was our turn. We performed the movements, adding in our ripples, and with that pattern we won the gold. The first team medal for the USA.

In life, sports, and business, everything comes back to the basics. Chon-Ji, the first pattern that every white belt learns, was the pattern that earned Team USA its first team gold medal. It wasn't the fancy kicks or the strength that helped us win. It was our commitment to learning the fundamentals, conquering the grind, pushing through that last month when everyone was tired to give it our all, which won us that tournament.

It's the same in business. Everything comes back to Chon-Ji.

CHAPTER 11

ORGANIZATION = PRIORITY + PLANNING

Bill Lee

In the previous chapters, we have discussed several examples where prior preparation made a huge difference in both career and athletic pursuits. To many, however, the idea of putting in so many hours of preparation before getting started seems impossible, especially given all our other responsibilities. That's where organization becomes a key concept in chasing excellence.

It is said that the great UCLA basketball coach John Wooden was so emphatic about organizing his practices that, at the beginning of every year, he would bring his team together and teach them how to put on socks. You heard me; he taught his college-aged players how to put on socks.

His method of putting on socks was designed to avoid creases, so that players could minimize the occurrence of blisters, and, in doing so, be that much quicker on their feet in a game. John Wooden won ten NCAA basketball championships in a twelve-year period, including seven in a row. He understood the importance of the little things, and despite all of his other responsibilities as a coach, he made sure that even something as small as putting on socks was taken care of correctly.

We have all had those moments when we feel like we are drowning in a sea of responsibilities. We have commitments to work, family, friends, and ourselves that we can't afford to neglect. Moreover sometimes those little things fall through the cracks, and we end up with painful blisters. What will become more and more obvious in your quest for excellence is the need to be precise about how you organize every aspect of your personal and professional life. Only through organization can you hope to meet your obligations in a manner that affords you the time and the opportunity to "go beyond."

I won't pretend to be an expert on organization. My mind is usually thinking of many different things at once, making it hard to act on any of them. But I've learned over the years that nothing can be accomplished without being organized, and I credit some of my most successful deals to knowing how to properly manage my time and be prepared before the deals actually surfaced.

Organization is a two-part equation that requires equal parts priority and planning. The first step, an essential when chasing excellence, is prioritizing everything in your life. This will require some thought and self-examination on your part. Here's how you do it, and you'll see it's not as hard as it sounds.

First, consider making a list of everything you spend time doing on a daily basis. This should include the tasks you perform at work, the time you spend with family, hobbies, interests, TV time, chores, and responsibilities. Nothing is too small. Include your meals, phone calls, information gathering, etc., and make sure to note how much time you spend on each item.

Next, organize these things by their importance to you. When you compare the two lists, you might make some pretty surprising discoveries. For example, maybe watching television ranks low on your list of priorities, but you spend more time sitting on the couch than you do catching up with old friends. These are the kinds of inconsistencies you want to be on the lookout for. This process will open your eyes to the small, inconsequential things you waste time on. And we all have them.

The next step is to consciously minimize the time you spend on those activities of lesser importance. Once you get rid of them, you will free up hours to pursue the vital things in your life, the things you prioritized to the top of your list.

The second part of organization is planning. It's one thing to make a resolution to spend more time with friends and less time watching television, but when you come home from a long day of work, you're more inclined to lie down, relax, and pick up the remote than you are to call up a buddy to go out for dinner.

When you have your priorities down, the only way to ensure you make time for the important things is to plan ahead. All it really takes is fifteen minutes of thought a day to ensure you are prepared. Make sure your plans are realistic, however; the goal is not to bite off more than you can chew but to manage your time wisely. This includes scheduling time to relax. Try taking a leaf out of Craig's book and schedule your naps into your daily calendar. With your list of priorities in hand, use the time available to you to plan for the things you said really matter in your life.

When you look at it this way, organization is like keeping your closet clean. How easy it is to just throw your clothes on the chair, and then, suddenly, a mountain of "stuff" grows in your bedroom? But if you plan ahead, and have a designated space to throw those dirty clothes, and a designated time for laundry and organizing your room, your life will become a lot less cluttered.

With notepads on our cellphones, remembering the little things is easier than ever. But with the growing responsibilities that come with chasing excellence, organizing and planning for those little things is also more important than ever. If you make conscious decisions about how you spend your time, you will master the journey toward excellence.

Another key thing about organization is that it allows you to be prepare for the unknown. You know your niche in CRE. Your business plan is based on your specific knowledge of a market segment. Your support information—graphs, charts, contact letters, resume, market profile, vision, etc.—should all be prepared and modified regularly so that at a moment's notice you are ready and not scrambling if something unexpected happens.

I'll give you an example. One Friday afternoon, just after lunch, I received a telephone call from the real estate manager at NCR, Scott Epling. Scott was calling me from his office in Dayton, Ohio. I had represented NCR five years previously in their lease and then sale to Prologis, of a 125,000 square foot industrial production facility in Ogden, Utah.

Scott was calling to see if this facility could be made available for lease, remembering that the lease we made on the premises was coming up and that the facility fit his need both in size and type.

I immediately placed a call to the current tenant and in one of those rare, perfectly-aligned moments discovered that they were not going to renew their lease. I called Scott back right away, and he told me he wanted to see the building on Monday morning.

I was all the way out in California, but I immediately arranged for the tour and flew out to meet with him and three other associates in Ogden that Monday. At the tour of the facility they told me that they were going to Las Vegas the next day and Phoenix the following day to look at other alternatives for the same requirement with two different brokers.

When it was immediately apparent that the Ogden facility would not work, as the majority of the manufacturing improvements had been removed, I asked if I could arrange for one of my associates to provide a summary of alternatives to support their other brokers in each city. Reluctantly, they said that that would be acceptable but it would have to fit into an already-full timeline.

I immediately called agents whom I trusted in both markets and on that Wednesday our Phoenix agent showed them one building that our competitor had missed. And it just so happened that it was the right building.

A month later I was invited to the lease signing in Phoenix. At that gathering, Scott told me that he was getting ready to sell a building that his company occupied in Brea, CA, my back yard. I sold, and then leased, that facility six months later.

Because I was organized and prepared with my business, I was able to quickly move things around to fly to Ogden, Utah and look the client in the eye. From there, I was able to gain a better understanding of the opportunity at hand and connect the client with our agents in Las Vegas and Phoenix. Our agents gave a good account of themselves because they were already fully invested and organized within their markets before they were aware of the opportunity at hand.

The point of the story is that the preparation was in place for this exact opportunity, even though we didn't know of it until the client called. If we hadn't done the work, understood the market, and been completely organized ahead of time, we all would have been scrambling when opportunity came knocking; but because we were prepared, we were able to respond quickly and efficiently.

CHAPTER 12

KEEP YOUR QUIVER FULL

R. Craig Coppola

What's the worst thing that can happen to an archer? He runs out of arrows.

What's the worst thing that can happen to a broker going into a meeting with a potential client? He runs out of material.

In either scenario, if you aren't over-prepared, you're screwed.

Bill's story in the previous chapter is a great example of preparation, but have you ever experienced being unprepared? The cost can be devastating. That's why preparation is the name of the game, and when you go into an important meeting or presentation, you should never run out of arrows. By this I mean you should never run out of items to discuss, no matter what happens during the presentation.

You never know in any meeting what direction it will go. Mike Tyson once said, "Everybody has a game plan until I punch them in the face."

This saying certainly pertains to the boxing ring, but it also rings true in meetings. You can go into a meeting thinking it will take one direction with one outcome, only to march down a different path with an entirely different outcome. You want to be prepared for anything, and have your arrows in your quiver for best-case and worst-case scenarios. You never want to be caught off guard.

That means preparing ahead of time, stocking up on arrows, and bringing everything you could need. If you have truly prepared thoroughly, it is unlikely you will ever have to use everything you have. My team and I go into every meeting with more arrows in our quiver than we ever use. We might go into a meeting with fifteen items and only use two or nine; we never use them all. The unused ones we put back in our quiver to bring out another day.

This idea is sometimes difficult for new members of our team to grasp. Multiple times I've had new runners put in hours of work compiling our fifteen items for a meeting. When the meeting ends, they want to keep pulling out the leftover items, saying, "And we have this ... and this ... and that ..."

They did the work, they have the fruit of their labor, and it's natural that they want to share it. Natural, but how powerful it is to save those items for another day. Every transaction has a moment when you need to fire off an arrow. And you need to fire the right arrow at the right time. You never want to give it to your prospect up-front, and you don't want to offer it too late. You also never want to show up empty-handed. It's a process. Sometimes you might not even have to shoot that arrow. It's all about timing.

For example, on initial tours, a site's location, quality of space, and parking ratios are key aspects. Once you get into the finals of the negotiation, after-hour air conditioning, tenant rosters, load factor of the building, and other things will become important. Each part of a lease negotiation has its season. You can't give everything up-front or you won't have anything to give or discuss later on.

Case in point: Not long ago I took my new runner to tour a client around one of our buildings. At the beginning of the tour, the runner handed the delegation the entire package we had put together, everything we were going to cover over the next hour. He gave it to them up-front, so that during the tour, we couldn't strategically present documents at the moment they seemed interested. Instead, the clients had all the information, so they didn't need to pay attention. We had nothing to discuss at the end of the tour.

What I normally do is create copies of each item and hand them out at the appropriate place in the tour. This keeps the client's attention and emphasizes the important things as we hit them. It also gives us more flexibility if the client wants the tour to go in a different direction.

Like an archer, you should over-prepare. Always have arrows in your quiver. However, archers never go out of their way to use them all. They save them for another fight, adding to them over time.

You should, in the same way, go ahead and over-prepare for every meeting, never run out of materials to bring to the table, and never force all your cards on the client at once. Never run out of arrows.

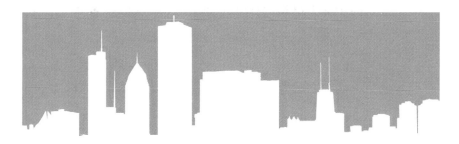

CHAPTER 13

GAYLE GOODRICH
GOT IT RIGHT

Bill Lee

Both organization and preparation require one other key term: discipline.

"Discipline" is such an easy word to say, and yet so hard to put into action. It's especially difficult to stay disciplined every day for years. Still, you won't realize a level of self-actualization without it. Think about it. Getting in shape requires discipline, and we all can probably identify with the difficulty of sticking to a diet or a workout regimen, whether it is for health reasons, weight loss, or bulking up. Academics require discipline for achievement and advancement in school. And when you add sports, fun, work, and relationships into the mix it becomes even harder to commit to everything.

Discipline, by my definition, is having the motivation to accomplish something that you really care about, and aside from your family, what is more worthwhile than caring about succeeding in your chosen profession? Remember how we talked about committing to commit? Committing is only half of the journey. Now you need the discipline to back it up. And by discipline, I mean hard work.

Individuals who back up academic achievement with extracurricular endeavors learn to manage time. They become disciplined on multiple fronts and are able to move forward successfully in doing so. It's no wonder some of the best brokers are individuals who mixed academics with sports or other extracurricular activities.

Athletes know how to dedicate themselves to a goal; they have the ability to focus, to learn new skill sets, cope with a rigorous schedule, and push themselves. They feel a great sense of accomplishment working through pain to reach a new level of personal excellence.

In high school, I used to walk by the local public school, the largest in the Los Angeles public school system, every day on my way to class at a Catholic all-boys school up the block. Every Saturday and Sunday, I would go to the public school gym and play pick-up basketball games with its players.

One of the players in that high school was Rich Levin, the leading scorer in the City of Los Angeles. He, along with another student Gayle Goodrich, received a basketball scholarship to UCLA. They graduated from high school just six months after me, and I followed their journeys very closely.

Levin went on to become the lead assistant to the commissioner of Major League Baseball, but Goodrich was the one who truly shined in the sport of basketball.

As a junior in high school, Goodrich, all five-feet-nine-inches of him, was an average player. He had neither height nor strength, but he played a decent game. As a senior in high school, he was very good; good enough to win Los Angeles City Player of the Year as his team won the city championship. He committed to UCLA, and though he wasn't their prize recruit, he still managed to get a scholarship and enjoyed success on the freshman team.

During his four years at UCLA, he got better every year. While he was there, UCLA took home two national championships, with Goodrich playing a key role in that success and becoming a first-team All-American player. When he graduated, he was a first-round draft choice; he played for the L.A. Lakers (by this time, six-foot-one-half-inch); and years later, he was named one of the all-time, fifty best basketball players in the history of the NBA.

Even though he was ranked as one of the top fifty players of all time, if the ranking was done by physicality, Goodrich would be in the bottom 10 percent of the 10,000 or so players drafted from college to play in the NBA. So how did he accomplish such a level of excellence with a body that wasn't particularly fast, definitely not very strong, obviously not tall, with a below average vertical jump, and nothing but quick reflexes to speak for him? It's very simple: he had the discipline to work hard, perhaps more discipline than anyone else.

Goodrich spent his high school and college years preparing for the NBA. He never let his lack of natural, physical ability stop him from pursuing his dream. He devoted his life to improving, and over time that discipline became a way of life. It became a habit that led him to be known as one of the best players in the history of the NBA.

Natural talent is nice to have, and sometimes it can get you pretty far. But without discipline and the ability to work hard and push yourself, you will eventually hit a brick wall. To experience real results, you have to cultivate the discipline to work hard, day in and day out, without fail. And when you feel the urge to push something off until tomorrow, to stop short of your goal, don't do it. It's as simple as that. Discipline is all mental. Be tough with yourself.

When you commit to discipline, sticking to it gets easier every day. Discipline breeds discipline until it becomes a habit. Embrace discipline, embrace the hard work.

CHAPTER 14

PAY THE MAN AND CONQUER THE GRIND

R. Craig Coppola

One of my true passions in life is backpacking. My goal every year is to spend thirty nights on the ground because I love hiking and camping. Every year, a few buddies and I plan ultra-long-distance hiking trips where we conquer some of the world's most beautiful and most challenging hikes.

Over the years I've been to some amazing places including New Zealand, Argentina, Peru, Chile, and Italy. But the trip that impresses most people is my trip to Mt. Everest.

My buddies and I decided we wanted to hike to the base camp of Everest, and climb some of the surrounding mountains in the Himalayas, the world's most formidable mountain range. I never harbored a desire to actually summit Everest because that trip is time-consuming and turns out to be more of a climb than a hike. Climbing is fine, but my true enjoyment comes from getting out of the matrix. So we were perfectly content with making it to base camp, as that hike is an accomplishment in itself. Also, base camp is really cool.

Not only were the trail logistics tough, but the months of training leading up to this hike were time-consuming. This trip required a lot of preparation. To get ready for the altitude, I would drive up to Flagstaff, Arizona, where the altitude was much higher than in Phoenix, where I lived. I then wore an oxygen-deprivation mask while I hiked, to train my lungs for low oxygen. I was on the trail every morning before work, putting in long hours of training for months before we left.

Whenever I train for something big, like the hike to Everest, I call it "paying the man." The concept is exactly what it sounds like. In life, if you want to buy something, you have to pay for it. For example, if you want to buy a car you have to pay for it, or set up some kind of payment plan to pay a little each month. There is no credit card for training. You have to pay up front before the event because if you don't, you will pay during the trip and, many times, not accomplish what you set out to do.

Training for a marathon or an ultra-long-distance hike is the same thing. If you want that end goal, if you want to run a marathon, you have to pay the man a little bit each day. Paying the man could be waking up early to run an hour, with each hour another payment you put toward that end goal of the marathon.

Paying the man works in business and life, too. You could pay the man by staying an hour later to cold call, and each call would be just one more step toward landing that big transaction. Whatever your end goal, you have to devote time every single day to pay the man in order to build up to success.

But putting in that extra work is a grind. It's not easy to wake up early to hit the gym, or skip the weekend football game to spend time working on a presentation for Monday. That's why to pay the man you have to "conquer the grind."

Conquering the grind is a daily commitment to overcome obstacles and excuses to make your daily payment. It's disciplining yourself to ignore the voice in your head that wants to sleep in, and hit the treadmill every morning. It's about putting in that extra work to make yourself stand out as someone who is truly excellent.

One way this plays out in commercial real estate is through the standard practice of driving the market. It's one thing to get on Google Maps and research an area, but you won't learn everything you need to know about the market you're working in until you get in the car and drive around.

Every Saturday for the first ten years of my career, I would wake up early and drive Phoenix. It was one of my precious days to spend with my kids, but it was the only time I could take out of my week to really get to know the area. So I got up early!

One morning, while I was in an industrial park in Phoenix, my car broke down. This was before I drove a nice car, back when my kids were still little. I had to call my wife at 5:45 a.m. and get her to load three sleepy kids in the car to come pick me up. But the next Saturday I was back at it with my engine fixed and ready to go.

We all have to pay the man in order to understand our market. If I hadn't taken that extra time to physically drive and get to know new neighborhoods and buildings, I would have never gained the knowledge or expertise I have today.

I still get up at 3:30 on Saturday mornings, but not to drive the market. Now I have the deep knowledge gleaned from working in my market for decades. Instead, I spend my Saturday mornings, not sleeping in or relaxing like most people, but working. I work from 4:00 a.m. to whenever I have something going on that day. For example, when my kids were growing up, I would work until they had a sports game. If nothing was going on, I worked until noon, when I had clocked in eight hours for the day. Then I would roll back into the house, where my teenagers would just be getting up from their weekend snooze, and spend the afternoon with them.

It's a grind. I don't enjoy waking up early Saturday mornings to work. I would much rather sleep in or go for a hike. But in order to pay the man, I have to conquer the grind every day, even those coveted weekend mornings. I still put in that extra work on Saturdays because I have experienced the immense difference that extra time makes on my workflow. And guess what? It pays off—in spades.

The average broker puts in forty or fifty hours per week to be just that: average. Anyone who puts in more than fifty hours can get ahead. Put in sixty hours, seventy, and you'll leave the competition in the dust.

That's not to say you should become a workaholic and give up everything else in your life. I have a steady balance of the most important areas in my life, including my wife, my kids, my athletic hobbies, and my other passions. I don't want to just be excellent in business, but in all areas of my life, and that means allotting time to work on those areas. Which, in turn, often means maintaining that 3:30 a.m. wake-up call.

You may listen to my story and shake your head, thinking that you couldn't possibly do the same thing, wake up that early or work that late and still have time for everything else. But if you are truly efficient with your days, plan your time wisely, and cut out extraneous things that are draining your time and energy, you'll be surprised at what you can accomplish with your 168 hours a week. But only if you conquer the grind and pay the man every day.

CHAPTER 15

THE TWO TYPES OF PAIN

R. Craig Coppola

Conquer the grind and pay the man—easier said than done, right? How do you conquer the grind when you're on your fifth straight hour cold calling? How do you pay the man when you got almost no sleep the night before?

Whether you realize it or not, every important decision comes down to a choice between two types of pain: the pain of discipline and the pain of regret. Which one you choose will determine your future, and whether you will successfully conquer the grind and pay the man.

The pain of discipline is the pain that occurs in the moment. It's the grogginess you feel when you wake up early for that run. It's the reluctance you have when you are starting your cold calls. It's the cramp in your back when you reach hour twelve of sitting at your desk working on a presentation. The pain of discipline is the pain that begs you to sleep for five more minutes, put off that run until tomorrow, check your emails before you start canvassing, or pick up your work tomorrow in the morning.

The pain of regret is pain associated with long-term disappointment and failure. It's when you kick yourself for being late to the office after oversleeping. It's the disappointment when you check the scale and don't see the number you want. It's when you don't make the call and the tenant shows up for a tour with another broker. The pain of regret lasts far longer than the pain of discipline, and its consequences are far more extensive.

The choice between the pain of discipline and the pain of regret is not easy. In the moment, the pain of regret seems so enticing, a much easier burden to bear. "I can run tomorrow; today, sleep is what I need," you think. Then you wake up and regret that you gave in to your own laziness. That's the pain of regret, and it feels horrible. The pain of regret grows over time and weighs you down. It strips you of your own self-esteem and robs you of your confidence. The pain of discipline, on the other hand, is short-term. *Ugh; peeling back those covers and walking to the closet to get your running shoes is so hard!* But in truth, by the time you get your running shoes on and stretch for a few minutes, that run seems like a pretty good idea. The pain of discipline is so strong in the moment, but so fleeting.

Once you understand the two types of pain and you can recognize them in your life, you are well on the path to taking control of your own destiny. The pain of discipline is often hard to overcome. But know it is momentary. The pain of regret seems like a no-brainer, but in truth it can be life diminishing, self-esteem robbing. I say avoid it at all costs.

In my life, I've found the pain of discipline is always better than the pain of regret, simply because it doesn't last nearly as long. Waking up in the morning is hard, and yes it is much easier to press "snooze" for five more minutes, but once I'm out of bed it's over, the pain of discipline is gone. The pain of regret upon being late to the office or not having time to prepare for the day properly lasts much longer than that split second it takes to throw aside the sheets.

Most people agree with this, but still find it difficult to get out of bed. That's why discipline is one of the most important parts of life. Learning how to overcome momentary pain and motivate yourself to do what you have to do will almost always guarantee you success.

Discipline is what gets me up every Saturday morning to get in four or more hours of work. It may not sound like that would make much of a difference, but do the math: it turns into sixteen hours a month, 160 hours a year, 4,800 hours in my thirty-year career of additional work that I would definitely regret not having. It puts me ahead of the game. Ahead of my competition. And I don't miss anything by doing it because I have disciplined myself to get up early and get the work done.

Like anything else, I had to train myself to make getting up early a habit. But other times, the pain of discipline was not easy to overcome. I used to be an ultramarathon runner. But there have been marathons I've participated in that I wasn't in shape for. My first hundred-mile run turned into a fifty-two-mile run because I had to drop out halfway through. I wasn't prepared for the race because I had let the pain of discipline get the better of me during my training. I had to deal with the pain of regret from not finishing that race for a long time.

In the end, though, I found a constructive way to deal with that regret. I turned that pain of regret into the motivation I needed to overcome the pain of discipline the next time I trained for a hundred-mile run. I didn't want to ever feel the way I felt after that race again. Period. That got me training with discipline, with a vengeance. I have never dropped out of a race since.

In business, the pain of discipline manifests itself in so many ways, big and small. One way is in cold calls and canvassing. In the moment, many brokers are reluctant to drive around, stopping into offices and making calls in person. Canvassing is not their idea of a good time, and they feel they could be spending those hours being much more productive in the comfort of their own office. But the satisfaction of canvassing and getting a solid lead will last you far longer than the potential awkwardness of walking into a meeting with someone you don't know.

Remember that the pain of discipline is momentary, but the pain of regret lasts some people their whole life. The next time you face a difficult decision, think it through and ask yourself honestly which one you can really handle. Then choose the momentary pain of discipline. This is the answer. It will change your life.

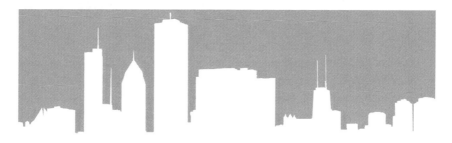

CHAPTER 16

STICK VS. CARROT

R. Craig Coppola

Motivation goes hand in hand with discipline, and it occurs two different ways. Chances are you've heard the saying "stick versus carrot" sometime in your life. It refers to the fact that motivation happens either through punishment (the stick) or rewards (the carrot). I wonder why they didn't change carrot to something like "chocolate chip cookie?" In any case, the stick and the carrot are two completely opposite methods of achieving excellence for yourself and helping others to achieve excellence, too. I know I have heard this phrase in reference to parenting, economics, politics, history, sports, business, and much more.

If you read leadership books or ask leadership gurus, the general consensus is that the carrot is better, right? People perform better if there is some type of incentive for their efforts. They perform out of the promise of a reward for excelling, rather than fear of punishment for doing something wrong. In fact, the general consensus is you want to take risks and fail, so that you can learn and grow in your career and profession. Harsh punishments, people say, can be incredibly demotivating. The thinking is it might cause people to not even try. "After all, why bother? Nothing I do is going to be good enough," they believe.

I fully agree that you need the carrots to inspire and motivate people toward excellence. The carrot, when you think about it, is the driver of entrepreneurism, the reason most people get up and go to work in the morning. And every entrepreneur's carrot is different. For some, the carrot may be about money. For others, the carrot is about changing the world. And for others, the carrot is about building something and watching it grow. Of course there are many other carrots, too, but the common theme is that there is an award worth fighting for. The carrot is really a homemade chocolate chip cookie! Or maybe it's a bigger paycheck, a bonus, or something else to inspire the kind of hard work and drive toward excellence this business takes.

Over the last couple of years, I've discovered that to be truly efficient, to fully pursue excellence, I need sticks, too. Carrots alone are not enough. That's why my team and I have sticks in place for those times when we don't perform or we fall short. They are consequences that help prevent poor behavior. The stick concept sounds harsh; it has an almost primitive and barbaric connotation. But it doesn't have to be like that. Sometimes the stick is just a rule you put in place for when you don't achieve your goal. It serves as an extra layer of motivation.

For example, my team sets goals for the number of cold calls we want to make per month. If we don't reach our goal, then everyone on our team, including me, has a dollar amount to pay. If we don't succeed, we each write a check. We call it "Stick Management." Other people I know impose fines for being late to meetings or for having cell phones ring or buzz during meetings. The idea here is to ensure that full respect of others' time and attention becomes the norm.

The stick strategy works. It has motivated the team to work together in order to avoid the given consequence. And the friends I know who impose the meeting rule penalties report the same thing. I tried the carrot on its own a long time ago, and in some areas of the business it worked great. In other areas, not so much. Sometimes you need the threat of the stick to give you that extra push to achieve.

As my friend, Dr. Chris Croner, founder of Sales Drive, points out, one of the key performance indicators of top salespeople is the need for achievement. That can be a carrot or a stick. In my pursuit of excellence, I never lose stick management goals.

The carrot as a sole strategy is nice in theory, but I've seen that it can breed a level of entitlement and excuses. For one thing, when faced with a better carrot, it's all too easy to let the one dangling in front of you go. For example, let's say the incentive is basketball game tickets if you finish making a hundred cold calls. Then your buddy calls you and says, "Hey, I got tickets to the basketball game tonight. C'mon, call it a day early and meet me downtown for a beer and the game."

Without the stick it's very easy to ditch the carrot in front of you for this more immediate offer. How easy it becomes to convince yourself you don't need that other carrot? Life's too short, after all! You hightail it downtown for the game instead of staying late and finishing the work you need to do to get the reward.

And then there is the tendency of people to need bigger and bigger carrots just to catch their attention. The incentive of game tickets, for example, is not as lucrative once you've gone to a few games. The whole carrot system starts to break down purely through our own human tendencies. This is what I mean when I say the carrot strategy works well in theory. But in reality, it is simply not enough to save us from ourselves.

The stick saves us from our laziness. It saves us from temptation. It saves us from our boredom. The stick makes the important work we do a lot more important than our own desires. And when done right, the stick can be even more meaningful than the carrot. Consider a stick that involves not letting your team down or a stick that involves making sure your clients' needs are met and they are not disappointed.

With the stick, you give yourself a checkpoint that makes tasks that much more important. It's especially effective in teams, and you see the best form of Stick Management in sports. When a team has a bad practice or loses a game, coaches often assign extra drills. It's avoiding the "drop and give me twenty" reality that motivates athletes to perform at their highest level all the time. The rewards are great, too: a water break if you complete this drill successfully or a night off from practice if you win the game. But which would make you want to work harder, the promise of a water break or the threat of an extra ten laps at the end of practice?

Stick Management doesn't equate to total dictatorship. Life is all about finding balance, and a healthy mix of sticks and carrots will motivate you and your team to accomplish every goal you set. It takes both sticks and carrots to achieve excellence.

CHAPTER 17

HIGH FIVE!
I LOST BY LESS!

Bill Lee

Motivation comes from a variety of places. Whether the stick or the carrot, discovering where your motivation comes from is one of the most crucial things you can do when you chase excellence, because that will be what keeps you going when you are disheartened.

One person who has discovered a wholly unique method of motivation is Jeff Huberman. Jeff is a really positive guy, so much so that his nicknames growing up were "Sunny" and "Happy." Jeff is also one of the most successful brokers in our Southern California Lee offices. He is, in my opinion, a truly special person for many reasons: discipline, loyalty, honesty, integrity, consistency, humility, and I could continue on. He also likes to mark today's capability with his past accomplishments, meaning he loves to compete against himself—whether it's getting up fifteen minutes earlier this year than last, modifying his work-out regimen positively, organizing his family time more effectively, or adding to his business relationships. It's this competition against himself that acts as his main motivator.

"On a scale from one to ten," Jeff says, "I'm a level ten when I'm competitive with myself, and maybe only an eight or nine when I compete with other people. I just want to improve myself."

When Jeff was in college, he had a roommate named Cole who was a phenomenal runner. Cole could run 4-minute miles. Jeff had been an athlete in high school, but wasn't nearly as fast as Cole. They would get together and run laps at the university's track, setting up beer and pizza at the finish line as motivation.

Because he was so much faster, Cole would give Jeff a one-lap lead whenever they raced. But even with that lead, Cole would finish at least half a lap ahead of Jeff every time. But Jeff didn't mind losing. He wasn't really there to compete against his roommate. He was there because he was competing against himself. He loved closing the gap, diminishing the amount of time he lost by less and less. It was this competition against himself, beating his own time, that pushed him to work harder.

Most athletes find the ability to compete is an important skill that aids them in succeeding in business. I know I felt that way. I wonder, however, if it could also be a hindrance. Competition, while a measure of performance, is not always a measure of ability. So do you measure your success by your standing with others, or your ability to accomplish?

Commercial real estate offers endless opportunities for competition, but to me, the real opportunity is the platform it offers to self-actualize. Knowing that there are but a few Thomas Edisons, Albert Einsteins, and Steve Jobs in this world is one thing. But those of us in the CRE industry also know that we are blessed with the chance to sort through all aspects of our industry, an industry that affords us the opportunity for great wealth by thinking, planning, and initiating how we can separate ourselves from the pack by going where others have not. Wow, we are lucky people to work in this industry for a career.

When I came to the conclusion that it was not necessary to compete with others to be truly excellent, competing instead with myself, managing not just work but all aspects of my daily life, I felt a huge life change.

The idea of competing against yourself can be confusing for many. Most people believe you need to have some sort of opponent or enemy to beat in order to be competitive. But competitors who compete against themselves find themselves consistently improving themselves much faster than those who are in it merely to beat an opponent.

The goal becomes about how good I can be, rather than beating someone else or achieving some external goal. It's an inward process, one that never ends because you can always improve yourself; you can always do better. So if you're like me, and you live for the drive and for the competition, and you've decided to commit to this road to excellence, competing against yourself is one of the most exhilarating and successful ways to get there. It's the driving force behind the discipline you need to win. If you can learn to master this mindset, you will achieve an incredible amount of confidence.

There is always going to be someone better out there, and you might not always be able to beat them. Losing is inevitable in sports, just as it is inevitable in commercial real estate. But there's power in knowing that you can win against yourself, that you can push beyond your own records to get better and better.

As Jeff says, "To compete, you have to be prepared to fail." For many people it's easier to not try, to avoid failing by not even working for it. Rejection is a huge part of the business, and most people lose a lot before they win a few. Consider Kobe Bryant, one of the best basketball players in NBA history who recently passed the mark for having the most *missed* shots in the history of the NBA. Accepting failure as a part of life is a huge part of winning.

If you measure your success against others, it's easy to get discouraged when you lose. But by measuring your success against yourself, you will be better able to track your improvement, and sometimes that's exactly the motivation you need to keep going.

CHAPTER 18
THE TOMATO-GROWING CONTEST
Bill Lee

When you make your living in commercial real estate, it's an advantage to be competitive by nature. The drive for competition has stayed with me my entire life. Long after my body was unable to play competitive sports, I still felt a hunger for competition. Case in point: my life-long love affair with body boarding, a sport I shared with a group of buddies. They were all very successful men. One was an emergency room doctor, another was an antique dealer, and another worked for a Security Bank buying and selling currency.

One day in September, as we were all approaching our forties, we were bobbing in the ocean on our boards. With no swell, and little chance to catch a wave, we found ourselves talking about what we could do at our age to continue being competitive. Playing other sports after long years of wear and tear, knee surgeries, and early arthritis was becoming increasingly foolish for all of us.

We decided on a safer way to compete. We decided to have a tomato-growing contest, and whoever could grow the largest and best tasting tomatoes would win. None of us knew anything about gardening so it was a level playing field, a chance to really compete.

When I got home that day, I was fired up. Running into the house, my first stop was the bookshelf that contained my set of encyclopedias (Google didn't exist back then). I was determined to win this competition, so I had to do my homework. I went to the entry about tomatoes and then found myself reading the agronomy section. In that book, there was a picture of Jacob Mittleider. He was shown growing tomatoes on the hillsides of Peru, and his story was that he could grow anything, anywhere. And what luck! This tomato expert lived in Salt Lake City, right here in the United States!

So what did I do? I got his phone number through 411, called him up and got him on the phone. I told him about the competition I had going with my friends. He told me, "Bill, you're going to win the contest because I've written a book on grow-box gardening. Not only that, I've also written a book on growing tomatoes. Not only that, I have packaged minerals that I use for my garden that I can send you right now."

I couldn't believe my luck! He stayed true to his word and mailed me all the stuff I needed to start my own grow-box garden of tomatoes. I followed his instructions carefully and within a few months, I had the tallest and most productive tomato plants among all my friends. My plants grew so tall, my neighbor called the homeowner association on me because they blocked her view of the ocean.

Needless to say, I won the competition, but of course my pals would never admit to it. But I didn't stop gardening there. That competition with others led me to a competition with myself as I continued to experiment with new plants, and to this day I still bring sacks of fresh tomatoes to all my friends whenever I visit. A huge patch of my yard is taken up by all kinds of different crops. I've challenged myself to grow my gardening knowledge and expertise over the years. It's become something that I love.

Thirty years later, I still have a competition with myself to see if I can grow not only a really strong tomato crop, but a yard full of other vegetables, berries, and fruit trees as well.

The drive to compete against yourself never goes away. People quit sports; they lose their ability to play; they find themselves without other competitors. But you will always remain your biggest competitor. You can always find areas to push yourself to be better in. It doesn't just have to be business or sports. It can be anything, even gardening.

PLATFORM PROFILE
John Cushman (Cushman & Wakefield)

John, growing up in the greater New York area (Montclair, New Jersey), is part of a seven-generation commercial real estate family, so imagine the dinner table conversations that took place for him in his youth. John is an unparalleled dealmaker across the country, and now internationally, and is still going strong at age seventy-three. I admire his confidence, tenacity, competitiveness, knowledge, and excellence.

I also admire his fearlessness; he left the comfort and familiarity of New York to come out West and captain the Arco Towers office project, the largest listing opportunity in the world at that time, consisting of 4,300,000 square feet of gross floor area. In doing so, he not only built the Cushman Wakefield presence in the West, but he also leveraged the opportunity into the best platform that I've ever been made aware of in the industry. This platform is one of creating a focused business plan oriented to regular dialogue with Presidents, Board Members, and CEOs of our nation's largest companies. He attributes the relationship(s) he made with Atlantic Richfield (ARCO), now British Petroleum, through five CEOs, as the basis for formulating this business plan, which has led to his participating on the Board of Directors for fourteen major public companies.

He left C&W to prove a point and in doing so created another wonderful firm, Cushman Realty, which eventually merged with Cushman Wakefield after achieving twenty-three years of great success. John was an innovator at Cushman Realty, a leader at Cushman & Wakefield (Chairman/Co-Chairman since 2003), and as fierce and knowledgeable a competitor as there has ever been in the industry. Scouting has been part of his life since his days as an Eagle Scout as a youth, to eventually becoming the National President of the Boy Scouts of America. He attributes scout sayings "do a good thing daily", and "be prepared" as fundamental to his life while also recognizing the leadership qualities he gained by being around Scoutmasters like the Treasurer of Standard Oil. He also believes, as a former military man, in "giving back to your Country"; whether it be service, volunteering, mentoring, participating, or through generosity. If there is one take away about how he chased excellence it would be his belief that you always have to be 'on point', meaning absolutely on top of all issues related to the opportunity at hand.

The newer Cushman & Wakefield/DTZ platform starts with great name recognition. C&W has historically been viewed as the number one office firm in the nation, particularly in New York, this nation's and maybe the world's largest, office market. And now John, through the DTZ merger, can access six continents and sixty countries with 43,000 employees to advance his brokerage excellence.

SECTION III:
REFINE EXCELLENCE

CHAPTER 19
EXCELLENCE IS CONTAGIOUS
R. Craig Coppola

If there's one thing I've discovered over the years, it's that excellence can't be contained to just one area of your life. When you embark on this journey to excellence, you have to, at your deepest level, embrace excellence not only in your work life but also in everything you do. Bill and I wrote this book with commercial real estate brokers in mind, but the topics and lessons we discuss are applicable to all people and in all parts of their lives. So your journey becomes chasing excellence in business, in relationships, in hobbies, and so much more.

Now that might sound like more than you signed on for when you picked up this book, but once you get started on this path, you'll see excellence is contagious. The determination, the commitment, and the discipline required to chase excellence at the office can't be turned off when you get home. It doesn't work like that. Your journey to excellence is destined to change you, so face it and be ready. It's an exhilarating ride and, believe me, once you fully commit to it you can't and won't settle for average in any other area of your life.

As I mentioned earlier, my path to excellence began with a thirst for accomplishment. I began by chasing one goal, which evolved into a constant pursuit of awards and recognition. That's just who I was, perhaps who I still am. I worked my tail off in my first decade with the goal of being the top-producing broker in the company, pushing myself to win again and again. When I made the choice to pursue something more, to chase excellence, I quickly realized that this choice wouldn't be contained to the baseball world or the business world. I started chasing excellence in all areas of life, driven by the quest for "more." In my case, that "more" was achievement.

I have a unique concept that helps me stay on track toward my journey to excellence. And it's a concept that works in the most important areas of my life. I've written about this idea in my own book, *The Fantastic Life*, but I'll give you a brief synopsis here.

To help me stay focused, I am constantly updating five different resumes. Most people will stop and reread that sentence. A resume? A list of your work and educational experience? And you have five of them? What the heck are you talking about?

Consider this for a moment. Why does a resume have to be *only* a place where you list your work history? Why can't it also serve as a record of your achievements and experience, as well as a measurement of your growth, in all areas of your life? Built properly, your resume can track your success as you acquire new achievements. Don't you feel pretty good about yourself when you add an accomplishment or new job title to your work resume? Why not apply that concept to other areas of your life?

That's why I maintain not just a business resume but also a husband resume, a father resume, an athletic resume, and a spiritual resume.

My goals for each are pretty simple. For my work resume, I focus on adding different types of deals, new clients, and accomplishments to my list. On my husband resume, I seek to deepen my relationship with my wife, and spend time together one-on-one (a challenge when you have four kids). For my father resume, I want to connect with my children on a personal level. As they've grown up and moved away from home, I strive to see them at least once every sixty days. Just last month, I flew to California for the day to have lunch and hike with my oldest daughter, before flying back home later that night.

My athletic and spiritual resume goals are equally as simple. I work on my athletic resume by spending at least thirty nights a year on the ground camping, and planning ultra-long-distance hiking trips with a few buddies of mine once a year. And my spiritual resume is about meditating every day, and making a connection with my faith.

I am adding to these resumes on a daily basis. Even if it's something small, like texting my son to let him know I'm thinking about him, or finding an hour a day to exercise, I consider it a win for my resume.

However, the goal of a work resume is to build on your knowledge, and to have a variety of experiences on there. You don't want a resume that shows the same type of job or same job level for the past thirty years. Rather, you want to show your promotions, your accomplishments, the things that demonstrate your growth and knowledge. You also want to add things that set your resume apart, that show you are unique. It's the same with your other resumes.

For example, on my athletic resume, I have finished tons of marathons. I ran marathons for years, setting and achieving goals such as qualifying for and running the Boston Marathon twice and breaking three hours. But after a while, I started wanting more achievement. I had participated in many of the nation's top marathons, and my career as a marathoner seemed to be very solid. But being the competitive person I am, I knew I wouldn't be content just running the same marathons over and over again. I wanted something bigger to put on my resume, something truly noteworthy that would set me apart. After all, a lot of people run marathons; I didn't want to be like a lot of people.

So I started running ultramarathons. First fifty miles, then one hundred miles (in one day), and then—I set my sights on the Marathon des Sables.

The Marathon des Sables is a three-day, 150-mile self-sufficiency race through the Sahara Desert. Sound crazy? That's because it is. This is considered the toughest footrace in the world. But I was chasing excellence, and this was my next step.

To prepare myself for the heat, I trained at noon every day in the middle of the Arizona summer, bundled up in sweatpants and a sweatshirt. I put in long hours of work and preparation until I finally made it to the actual race.

The Marathon des Sables lived up to its reputation. It was long, grueling, and hot. I returned home from the race chafed everywhere, exhausted, dehydrated, and cleaning sand out of every orifice in my body for two weeks. But it was worth it. I'd had an experience I knew very few people would ever have. I had accomplished something big that I'd worked toward for almost a decade, and added something impressive to my resume. I could begin turning my attention away from running and toward other athletic pursuits with an easy mind, knowing I had conquered my running resume.

What is the Marathon des Sables in your life? What's the next big step in your hobby, in your family life, in your sport of choice, in your spirituality, in your work? What's holding you back from pursuing it wholeheartedly? The journey to excellence in your career is not an excuse to let the other things in your life slide. Rather, it should be motivation to begin growing in those other areas as well, and adding to your resume of achievements. When you accomplish goals, find new ones, and let your drive take you through life. Twenty-five years later, my running resume has now become a resume for backpacking all over the world. I closed the door on one pursuit and opened another, bringing with me the same lessons and determination.

Excellence is contagious. You can begin with a singular focus, building one area of your life, but don't stop there. Let it spread from your career to other areas of your life and, eventually, other people in your life.

CHAPTER 20

EVERYTHING IS BEING DISRUPTED —EXCEPT THIS

R. Craig Coppola

As I've gained success and hit my thirtieth year in brokerage, I've started looking at my success with an eye toward my legacy. With two of my kids already out of college, and two more finishing up their education, I think back to finger painting and bedtime story days with fondness. I've never been one to fight change, but there's truth to the statement that things were simpler in the past. Well, maybe not simpler, but they were much more predictable.

Today, everything is being disrupted. Old business models and "the way we used to do it" mentalities are crumbling under the weight of new innovations. These days, disruption is the new norm.

What does this mean for businesses? In my experience, it means that there are no more sacred cows. "Sacred cows" refers to the Hindu belief that cows are holy beings and are never to be slain. In business, it refers to the traditions that companies cling to and refuse to slay or simply update, even though the times have changed. And unfortunately, the relevance of those traditions is quickly disappearing.

Today, there's no tradition that isn't on the table. Everything has to be up for grabs all the time. Change is the new normal, and you have to be willing to give up everything in order to keep up with the competition. Companies that cling to the old ways, to the methods that have worked for years, are being replaced by newer startups with fluid, adaptable structures; innovative ideas; and rapid implementation of those ideas. These more flexible competitors are coming in and stealing business from the companies that refuse to change. Everything, from client acquisitions to communications to corporate structure, is being disrupted.

The only thing that still stands, and I believe will continue to stand, is the notion of relationships. Relationships will always be the most important aspect of business because, even though the tools of relationship building continue to change, human connections are everlasting. There is nothing newer or better that will supplant relationships. Relationships will remain vital to business success, no matter what else changes.

The pursuit of excellence means learning to let go of the old and embrace the new. And believe me, there is a lot of new coming our way. You have to be okay with this or you will not survive in this business or any business.

Some tangible examples of the type of disruptions I'm speaking of include:

1. Technology. This is a big one. The way we access information has changed drastically over the past two decades. With the Internet, laptops, smartphones, and Google, every year the changes in this sector come faster and hit harder. While many of these changes are improving the way we do business, helping us work quicker and more efficiently, it can be difficult to keep up with the latest technologies.

   For brokers, a prominent example of technology disrupting the business is CoStar. Listings are now easy to access online. No more driving around and writing down the information on a leasing sign.

Today, everything you need to know about a building is a click away, making business much quicker and, as a result, much more competitive.

2. Companies chasing national accounts. JLL and CBRE are getting tons of national accounts, and they are taking on any company with more than fifteen to twenty offices nationwide. It used to be that they would only work with companies with more than fifty offices, but these days they're facing stiff competition from all the other brokerages that are chasing national accounts. The idea of working with national companies is growing increasingly prevalent in our industry.

3. Office space. This is a huge interest of mine. When I started out, the typical office consisted of as many gray cubicles as could fit in one space, a few conference rooms, and one or two offices with a view for the higher-ups. Today, open space concepts are dominating the markets. Communal workstations, cool cafés, lounges these are the new norm. These are what millennials entering the workforce are looking for in an office. If you want to attract new talent, you have to be open to new structures.

Is anything really sacred anymore? Can you honestly examine your industry, your company, and find something that you believe will never change? I've put my mind to it and the only true sacred cow that remains is relationships. Everything else is up for grabs to the fastest, brightest innovators. If you're not prepared to adapt, then be prepared to be left in the dust.

CHAPTER 21

HELP YOURSELF BY HELPING YOUR COMPETITION

Bill Lee

When I realized I no longer competed against others, that I competed against myself, I had a new thought: If I'm not competing against others, why don't I embrace them? Why waste my time fighting them when I could be supporting them, and making myself stand out? Our business can be very cutthroat and jealous, so you can set yourself apart pretty quickly by embracing your competitors.

When you compete against yourself, everything changes, particularly your mindset and the way you interface with other people. When you take the time to congratulate or encourage your competitors, they look at you and talk about you differently. It just happens and it is quite extraordinary.

"Brokering a deal is like dancing," says Tom Piernik. "You have to be in step with your partner, and sense what to do to get in step with another person."

Tom is an expert at this dance. He knows how to work with people, even assholes (his word, but of course it has encroached into my vernacular a time or two), to accomplish a deal that makes everyone happy.

Early in their careers, Tom and his partner, Dave Mudge, went up to Los Angeles and met with a competing broker named Chuck. Chuck represented Amtrak, and had just completed a 60,000-square-foot deal for his client. Tom and Dave wanted to find out about the deal so they set up a time to meet. When they met with Chuck, he asked them, "Why are brokers such assholes?" Chuck had needed information about a growth area he was unfamiliar with and almost every broker he'd contacted had been reluctant to share anything of value. They all fought against him, rather than help him make the deal happen. The reason, of course, is they didn't see any profit in it for themselves. I should probably say immediate profit.

At that moment, Tom and Dave had an epiphany. They decided not to fight these guys but to help them instead. From then on, they made a business out of being a resource for other brokers in their area. Providing information for other brokers became part of their business plan, and allowed them to achieve an incredible amount of success.

Tom says all brokers want and need to work with other brokers, but so many of them are too caught up in beating the other guy that they limit themselves by competing instead of cooperating. One broker cannot make all the deals, so cooperation is a good thing. Making good relationships and helping others comes back to you in the end.

Tom doesn't compete with brokers; he competes with himself. He openly shares information with other brokers in his own market. Tom's theory is simple: help other brokers be successful, and they will want to help you be successful. It might seem counterintuitive, but that theory has helped Tom make a lot of money.

When you compete against yourself, you stop worrying about what the other guy is doing and realize there's no need to be an asshole to your competitors. Concern yourself with your own deals and your own success and don't worry about the other guy getting more than you. Help the other guy get more than you and, believe me—and Tom—you will come out on top and make some great friends in the process.

CHAPTER 22

LONE WOLF NO MORE

R. Craig Coppola

Authors have dedicated entire books to the importance of relationships in business. And they likely say what everyone in business should already know: that building strong and long-lasting relationships is a cornerstone of success. But what those books may not tell you is, those relationships are vital to chasing that horizon known as excellence. Relationships take time to foster and time to keep, so it is important to invest in the right relationships. Whether you're helping out your competitor, or networking with a potential client, relationships are important to maintaining good life balance while you do good business.

The commercial real estate industry is constantly changing. What better way to keep abreast of these changes than networking with others in and out of your market? Building these relationships allows you a degree of stability, especially in tumultuous times. Creating links with like-minded, successful people that grow into mutually-beneficial relationships allows you to bring value to them, and the beauty of it all is that they often will do the same for you.

Networking is a difficult concept to teach. It can happen anywhere, anytime, which goes back to the idea of always being open and prepared. You can meet a potential business contact anywhere—at the office, the gym, or even the grocery store. Oftentimes, the most successful business relationships don't come into play until years after you've made the connection. You have no way of knowing which relationships will become important, which is why you have to be prepared to make contacts and grow those contacts into relationships everywhere you go.

Believe it or not, networking is giving. Too many people think of networking as an exercise in getting something out of other people. They make contacts with a "what's in it for me" mentality. But the people who are truly adept at building a network are the ones who give without expecting anything in return. They give favors, time, and resources freely, regardless of a person's status in a company or what they think they can get back. In other words, they are unselfish with their value.

Some years ago, an engineering firm needed to renew their space in Phoenix. I represented the building they were trying to renew, and worked on the deal on the listing side rather than the tenant side. On the client side, I found myself working with the office manager, a woman who knew nothing about real estate.

Her name was Jeanne, and she was a smart and interesting woman. I liked her right away, but it was clear she had never done this before. I decided to spend some time educating her about real estate and teaching her a few of the basics. She was interested in the industry, so I took time away from the deal to help her learn.

Jeanne ended up displaying a real passion for real estate. She loved it so much that she decided she wanted to start working on her company's real estate. She offered herself up to the corporate counsel to help with the company's real estate, and two or three years later she became the firm's Real Estate Director. This company had worked with a broker from a different national firm for years and they would call him when the need arose. But when Jeanne took the leadership post, she moved all the business to Lee & Associates and hired me right away to represent them.

Over the next few years, I did more than 130 transactions with HDR Engineering, one of the top five engineering companies in the world, all because I had helped one of their office managers learn the business. For the rest of her career, Jeanne and I maintained an incredible personal and business friendship.

Commercial real estate doesn't have to be a lone wolf endeavor. Maybe you are the main broker on a deal, or your name is on the sign outside the vacant building or even on the company door, but you cannot undervalue the importance of relationships to help you succeed. Over the past decade, solo brokers have been prevalent, but the best have always relied on others to compete and win, and you should, too.

CHAPTER 23

THE HUNDRED-DEGREE DEAL

Bill Lee

There are transaction people who make the deal, get their commission, get out, and never bother contacting that client again until their lease expiration approaches. The most successful brokers I know are nothing like that. Instead they are like Craig, building several important relationships such as the one he shared in the previous chapter. These brokers work with the same people and companies again and again because they've built and maintained trust from those that they have interfaced with. The people who can do this, who can sustain these relationships over years, decades even, are the ones who get business from all kinds of people in all kinds of places. Word travels fast. Business finds them, through renewals with the same clients, referrals to new clients, and in other serendipitous ways.

My second deal in the industry was with a company called Tempo Computers. When I contacted them, they were in the process of being purchased by GTE and needed eight acres of land to build a new industrial manufacturing factory. I approached its business leaders with a cold call and was told that they were working with other brokers in the area. I asked if I could bring them a few options as well.

New in the business, with no money coming in, a mortgage, and other bills to pay, I really needed to get this deal. I started doing my research; looking for properties that met their requirements, and found a few sites in the preferred area, including one large property that would be perfect for them should it be able to be divided.

About a week or so later, a representative from GTE came into town to check out their available options. His name was Jack Feeney and while I did not know it at the time, I later discovered that he was a legend in the industry, well-known among his peers. He was head of the GTE real estate department headquartered in Massachusetts, which included five other deal makers all reporting to Jack.

Jack came into town and we drove around to look at my properties. He recognized immediately that I was a rookie. But he was friendly, we talked sports, and he let me show him what I had—which was not exactly what he wanted.

Then I showed him a site that was not eight acres, but rather twenty-four acres, composed of three eight-acre parcels. It was in a good location and it was all owned by one man. Jack liked the property, and he told me he wanted to negotiate with the owner that same day, so later that afternoon we went out to the owner's house to meet with him.

The owner was a friendly guy and smart, a Stanford grad, who lived in a remote growth area of Southern California in one of those houses with a huge porch out front. As we were walking into the house, Jack turned to me and said, "Bill, I'd like to meet with him alone. Can you stay out here on the porch?"

Now, it was the middle of September, and about 100 degrees outside. But it was painfully obvious that I had little value to offer in this meeting, embarrassing, but true. So, with no choice other than to swallow my pride and wait, I sat out on the porch for the duration of the meeting, sweating in my suit and tie, while they negotiated the deal.

After about forty-five sweltering minutes, Jack finally came out with a big smile on his face. He had made the deal! GTE bought eight acres and optioned the remaining sixteen acres at a fixed price for the next six years.

But that meeting, and subsequent transaction, was only the beginning of the story. A few years later, while setting up cold-call meetings on the East Coast, and after frequent telephone calls advising Jack of the increasing value of the optioned land, I contacted Jack again and asked to visit him at the GTE headquarters. He brought me into their office, north of Boston, and introduced me to the other real estate managers on his team. All five of them!

These were active 'players' in the world of industrial real estate, people who transacted business all over the country, and most went on to become extremely influential in the industry. In that one meeting, I initiated five new relationships with people who, years later when they became directors for other companies, would call me to help them with their real estate requirements. At least one deal a year within that group of people happened for the next thirty years.

One of the biggest deals that came out of that meeting was with Frank Harvey. He later left GTE to become the director of real estate at Stanley Works. Stanley Works had a national contract with another brokerage firm, but because we had an existing relationship, Frank and I continued to do deals together over many years.

One day Frank called me up offering me the chance to do a big transaction. Stanley Works had to sell a property fast—by the quarter's end, which was less than ninety days away. Frank had another broker putting together an offer, but wanted to know what I could sell the property for within that time period.

So I did my research, put together my offer, and presented it to him. In the meeting, he said to me, "You know Bill, this other broker says that she can sell it for more."

Knowing that Frank's top concern was that this deal close at the end of the quarter, I didn't blink and replied, "I'm sure she does say that. But Frank, the market isn't that good right now, and I don't see a tenant for this vacant building on the short horizon. I'm the client in this deal. I'm putting this offer together for myself in a partnership with other investors. We are in a market where it is not uncommon for a buyer to renegotiate a purchase price during the contingency period. I can close within two days of receipt of the preliminary title report. You won't have to worry about a buyer you don't know renegotiating the deal. I can promise you I won't be changing my offer. You'll have a sure deal with me.

"But what I need from you is a short-term lease and a purchase money note for a year allowing me enough time to finance the deal."

And he agreed to do it!

So since I had been willing to swallow my pride and sit on a porch in the heat for forty-five minutes to help land a different deal many years back, I was able to build relationships with a group of real estate directors that led to a bevy of transactions for thirty years as well as the opportunity to purchase a property for myself.

There is no mistaking that deals like this happen because of the relationships you build over a long period of time. If you have a little humility, if you pursue these relationships with people, and recognize the value you have to offer and the value that they have to offer, you never know where your investment in others might lead you.

CHAPTER 24

GET PAID TOMORROW FOR A GOOD DEED TODAY

R. Craig Coppola

Bill's ability to maintain a long-lasting relationship, not only with his initial contact but with several others who emerged from that contact, is a rare strength. You'll find very few people who continue to call up old clients years after their last deal, and still get business from them. But if you can learn to master this skill, and learn to build strong, genuine relationships everywhere you go, hundreds of new doors and opportunities will open up to you.

I remember when I was a young broker in 1987, a call came out of the blue from a broker in New York. It was a young woman, and she said, "I'm looking for a property for an unnamed, East Coast-based company, and I need 10,000 square feet of medical space."

She had flown out to the area to drive around and get the lay of the land, but was getting nowhere. She was calling to see if one of my listings might work.

I said, "Look, let me help you. I know the market; I'll put a list together for you."

I had no idea who she was or what company she represented, but that night I put together a list of forty properties that met her specifications. We spent the next day driving through the properties and going over all my research.

She returned to New York and reported to her boss, a senior broker who was handling the actual negotiations. She said she got an education in Phoenix and realized that the firm didn't have the right people to handle this deal. She went back to the office and said, "We need to have someone local help us with this deal, and I think I found someone there who can work with us."

The senior broker wasn't convinced at first. He didn't want to bring in outside help; he wanted to take the whole commission for himself. With some persistence, I'm certain, she managed to convince him that they couldn't do this deal alone, and a few days later Sam Rozzi, the owner of Corporate National Realty in New York, called me up.

He said, "I hear I need to work with you."

At this point, I was a young guy, only three years into the business, and I hadn't expected to hear anything more from the woman I helped, let alone her boss. But Sam offered me the chance to work with him on the deal. He said, "We're going to split this client 50/50. You're going to handle the local stuff and I already have a great relationship with the real estate director of the company. So we will take it on together." What a tremendous opportunity for a young guy like me in the business.

It turned out that the company was Cigna, a global health insurance company. With that one deal I built a relationship not only with Cigna, going on to do thirty deals with them over a twelve-to-fifteen-year period, but also with Sam Rozzi, an incredibly successful and seasoned broker. Sam is still a great friend and partner who continues to invest in my own real estate deals, all because I took the time to drive one of his young brokers around.

By being generous and taking a little bit of time to help out other people, you can build a successful career that spans decades. So take the time to help others, even if you don't see any immediate profit for yourself. You never know where those relationships and good deeds will take you.

CHAPTER 25
DON'T BE OVERZEALOUS
Bill Lee

Commercial real estate is a business built on relationships, to be sure, but as I've said before, it's also a business for competitive people. It's for people who are practiced at always going for the win. But there's a fine line between being a winner and being overzealous. And that distinction can make or break the vital relationships you build in this industry.

I've known aggressive negotiators in my day; we all have. But then there are the overly aggressive negotiators, the overzealous ones. One broker I worked with years ago was at the top of the ultra-aggressive category. He topped the list. Make no mistake, his methods made him a lot of money. But they also made him a lot of enemies because he fought tooth and nail for every tiny detail, every tiny win for his tenant client. You might think that's a good thing; after all, he's working for his client, doing his job.

Maybe that's how he saw it, but the way the market saw it was much different. They saw it as a win-lose, take-no-prisoners approach, and his overly aggressive behavior burned a lot of bridges with landlords and other brokers. Big deal, you might think. But when ultra-competitive, ultra-aggressive behavior ends up damaging the tenant-landlord relationship—which it often does—that helps no one. After all, the client has to work in the building day in and day out. This broker was so insistent on having every detail, every dime, every concession go his way during the down markets that he, and his clients, often found themselves in a less than favorable position in up markets with their landlord.

Although this broker was very successful, he diminished his ability to create long-lasting relationships with tenants, landlords, and brokers. He was always searching for the next win. My point here is that when you negotiate, sometimes you have to look at the tenant or landlord you represent and say, "It's not in our best interest to get every last cent we can out of this deal." Tenants and landlords have to live with each other, so to preserve good relationships, you have to concede a little.

For competitive people, it's hard to give ground when you know you can win it all. But you bring more value to your clients by giving them counsel on the condition of the market and helping them build strong relationships on the other side of the table than you would squeezing everything you can out of a deal. Others might be happy just to book a deal, earn the commission, and move on, but that's not how you build a relationship. When you take the long-term perspective, you look beyond your one deal to potential future deals. Too few people take this perspective and too often your tenant, or landlord, have to revisit one another and ask for a favor.

The goal of excellence is not to just make money, though often that is one of the more positive side effects. The real goal of excellence is to be the best you can be. And a habit of excellence will help you succeed in all areas of life; it will help you stand out above the rest of the crowd of average people, and set yourself up for a lifetime of achievement. You can live a successful life, but without the respect or support of the people you work with, you will never achieve true excellence, nor will you maximize your true potential.

Real estate is a human business, a people business. It is made up of brokers, tenants, landlords, developers, architects, civil engineers, attorneys, accountants, contractors, etc., all of whom can help you in your career and life, both short-term and long-term, just as you can help them. That is a relationship.

And the best part is, you have the opportunity to develop friendships with the people you work with and gain a lot of value from them over many years—value that extends far beyond their commission potential. I have met some of my most cherished friends through the business.

Understandably, some business relationships will be transactions. There's no getting around it. And that's okay. You can still act with a relationship mindset—helping and cooperating versus competing—even if the relationships are a few months or ten years, depending on the length of the deals. Work like this and transactional relationships can repeat themselves for decades.

That leads me to an important point: you are not going to like everyone. But you can have a good working relationship with people you don't like. Especially early in your career, you'll find that you have to work with some people you don't like to get a deal done. But as you get older and more established, you can choose to do business with the people you genuinely enjoy being with. And those are the people you build human relationships with. You can co-op the transaction relationships with other agents.

I've known plenty of brokers who scoff at networking. Maybe it's because they are too obsessed with their own egos and have never developed the ability to form lasting relationships. Networking is contingent on your ability to be gracious, humble, and giving. No one extends themselves to those who don't give back.

If you find you aren't keeping the relationships you want or need, maybe it's time to reassess the way you treat your clients, associates, and friends. It's not hard to get with the program. Take the time to call up an old client you used to enjoy working with and see how he or she is doing. Invite an old business associate to lunch. It takes five minutes to check up on an old friend, and in those five minutes renew a friendship that could prove beneficial somewhere down the road. And here's the best part: you might just have more fun.

CHAPTER 26

THE DAMN FAX MACHINE

R. Craig Coppola

Years ago, I had acquired enough experience and market knowledge that I decided to start making my own investments in real estate. I wanted to build a personal portfolio and get some skin in the game. Like most endeavors I take on, I started by doing research. I spent weeks analyzing buildings in an area that I knew had great potential. I spent a lot of time analyzing properties and putting together a list of the top twenty ideal properties to buy. They were 10,000 to 40,000 square-foot buildings.

Thinking there was no time like the present, I started calling the owners of the buildings and simply telling them I wanted to buy their building. Even if they weren't willing to sell yet, I just wanted to start opening the lines of communication.

One building was perfect. It was the right size, had underground parking, and occupied a great location in Phoenix. And as fate would have it, I found out the church was interesting in selling—so I jumped on it.

The building was owned by a church, so I reached out to the person in charge of the disposition and started putting an offer together. Eventually, I became one of the final contenders for the deal. I spent a lot of energy and late nights arranging the transaction and building the relationship.

I faxed my final offer over to my contact on the day of the deadline (remember when we used faxes?), then sat around for a week waiting for the phone to ring. With each day that passed my heart sank lower and lower. Eventually, he called to tell me I didn't get the building. Someone else had bought it.

I was bummed out. I hated to lose, especially on this deal that had taken so much of my time and energy putting it together. Ninety days later the deal closed and the name of the buyer was made public. It was a man named Kern Schumaker, who had made a fortune buying real estate. Somehow he managed to give that church a better offer than mine and win the deal.

For years after, that deal haunted me. Every day driving to work I'd pass that building, always questioning what went wrong. Why was his deal better than mine? What mistake had I made?

Fifteen years later, I found myself in a meeting with Kern and some other business associates. After plucking up the courage, I finally turned to him and said, "You know, I never told you this, but you own that building down on Camelback Road. I was the other finalist to buy that building."

He just looked at me, smiled, and said, "Yeah, I know." I stared at him with some surprise. He said, "I knew you were the other finalist. In fact, I was sitting in the church office when your fax came in with your offer. I added $50,000 to your offer and made the deal."

Kern did more than just beat my offer. He beat me in terms of the relationship. He was the one who had the relationship with the church, not me, and it was because of that relationship that Kern happened to be sitting in the office on that particular day. That relationship got him the deal. It wasn't because he was a better businessperson or even that he had more money. That was when I realized that, in real estate, the relationship is far more important than the purchase price.

CHAPTER 27

LEADS ARE EVERYWHERE

R. Craig Coppola

In the business of commercial real estate, you can't survive on old business. Unlike other industries where companies become successful by doing work with the same clients over and over, brokers must always be chasing new leads. After all, how often can one company relocate? To stay ahead, you need to be constantly bringing in new business, from everywhere you can. This requires, you guessed it, a devotion to building relationships.

The process of chasing business, like chasing excellence, never stops. Thirty-plus years into my career, I still make fifty to one hundred cold calls a month, bringing in new leads. It's a never-ending process. But the thrill of the chase is what attracts many brokers to the business. So if you're a broker, there's a good chance you live for the sale. You're competitive; you want to win.

But for many new brokers, the ability to chase leads remains elusive. I know my runners take for granted the new deals I bring in. To them, I'm just a mystery guru at landing new deals. When they consider bringing in new business themselves, they suddenly falter.

"Who do you do business with? How do you find those leads?"

My answer is, "Everybody. All the time."

If you're in the business, you have to be in the business 24/7. Everyone you meet, talk to, or say hello to in passing is a potential lead. Every time you go to the grocery store, work out, or attend a basketball game, there is the chance to do business. Because business, especially commercial real estate, is about building relationships.

Most people turn their business self off when they leave the office. They believe that they shouldn't mix business life with personal life. But in commercial real estate, your business life should never stop. You should always be searching for new leads. You should always be thinking about how you can improve, even during your "time off." In fact, that's the best time to be working on your business, because it will get you further ahead than your competition every single time. Plus, often you're less distracted by the countless tasks of the day.

I've met clients while running in marathons, training for Tae Kwon Do, coaching Little League, serving on charity boards or performing charity work, while on vacation, even when dropping my kids off at a friend's birthday party. Each of these activities was seemingly far removed from my business, but instead of viewing the contacts I made at these events as social contacts, I also filed them under potential business contacts. Sure, nine times out of ten they remained simply friends or acquaintances. But it was that first contact that led me to a deal that made this way of thinking all worth it.

When my son was younger, he underwent physical therapy for a torn meniscus at a place called RehabPlus in Phoenix. The rehab center also doubled as a gym, so I would take my son every week and get in a workout while he was with his therapist.

During one session, I met a guy named Charlie Brewer, a personal injury attorney who was undergoing physical therapy for an arm injury. For the next couple of weeks, I'd see him and chat with him while he and my son did their exercises.

Years after our initial meeting, I had the chance to represent him in selling his building. Imagine that. We met at a rehab facility, struck up a few casual conversations, and ended up doing a deal together.

Leads come from everywhere. Never be shy about chasing business. View the world as one big opportunity rather than two separate spaces, business and personal. Even if you're with someone you would not typically consider a business connection, still consider him or her a prospect. You never know where those contacts will take you, or what kind of business they can bring you.

CHAPTER 28

IT'S MIGHTY CHILLY IN HERE

R. Craig Coppola

The most important and often the most difficult part of chasing new business is cold calling. This is the part that causes everyone to groan and roll their eyes. Yes, I know cold calling is not the most welcome or fun activity, at least not for most brokers (there are some who live for it, and you know who you are), but cold calling is a necessity in the business.

There's a vast difference between being open to receiving leads and actively seeking leads at all times. As we discussed in the previous chapter, you should always be chasing new business, and in this area the bread and butter of every broker is cold calling and canvassing (cold calling door-to-door, in person).

In the early days of my career, cold calling was literally that—sitting down, picking up the phone, and dialing my way through a long list of potential leads. Anyone who has had phone sales experience knows how the routine goes. You greet the person on the line, ask to be transferred, get a minute into your spiel, and meet with a cold, "No thank you." Maybe every once in a while you get someone interested in talking to you, but for the most part, you spend your days being thrown off the line.

Today, cold calling has evolved to include cold emailing as well as connections via social media. Your ability to make contacts is more varied than ever. But no matter the form, at the heart of cold calling should be the goal of creating strong, human connections. That's why, for my team, canvassing is one way to still chase leads because it allows you to make that contact and first impression in person and get to know the market at the same time. You create stronger, more personal connections when you take the time to physically seek someone out.

Which feels more personal to you? Receiving a call and listening to a speech someone has given twenty times that day, or having someone drop by your office and say, "Hey, I work nearby and would love to get to know you"? The answer is clear.

That's not to say cold calling and cold emailing aren't effective. There are many brokers who have made an art of reaching out to potential clients through technology. But never underestimate the power of a personal meeting and never forget that the road to excellence is about going above and beyond what "everybody else" does.

To be an accomplished cold caller/canvasser, you have to love interacting with people. And odds are if you're a broker, you already love meeting people. You know how to strike up a conversation, ask questions, and get people talking. It's typically part of the personality type this business attracts. The truth is, people want to work with people they like, so the sooner you can get people to like you, the better off you'll be. And the sooner you can get more and more people to like you, the better your business will take off.

Real estate, as I've said a hundred times before, is a business of people. Relationships are how you succeed. So if you are shy or introverted and are waiting for leads to come to you, spend some of that wait time getting over your fear. A good way to do that is to just get in the car and make a few stops. You'll mess up the first few times, but after the third or fourth stop, you'll get the hang of it. You'll change your business and you'll change your life when you do this. Eventually, you will start to feel so comfortable that you'll like it; you'll like the people and they will like you back.

When you take your interest in people and combine it with your discipline to make your calls or visits, cold calling becomes a numbers game with feeling. Make your calls, knock on the doors, and set up your meetings, every week, and when you do it, do so with empathy and passion. You have to meet people on their turf, not on yours. And you have to be doing it all the time.

As with everything else on this journey, the best way to measure your performance is to set weekly goals. For example, in my team we try to canvass three to twelve buildings per broker per month. When I get a new runner, I set the goal of twenty-five calls a week. We may not make our goal every month, but we always get something close to it.

Many brokers would laugh at my number, believing it to be unrealistic. For them, there simply isn't enough time in the day to keep up with that many calls and meetings. Plus, when you think about it, less than five percent of those calls turn into actual clients. Some brokers think it's a waste of time.

The average broker will cold call to get some new business, and then stop cold calling once he or she has landed a few deals. When the deals close, the broker will go back to cold calling until he or she gets another client. It's a cycle of call, get business, finish business.

But what happens if you get in the habit of making those contacts consistently, no matter your current workload? What happens if, while your colleagues have stopped calling to work on a deal, you're meeting a hundred new people that month? What are your odds of success, of getting business, compared to them? If you can stay on top of your goals and make those contacts constantly, you will never be left wondering where your next deal will come from.

After you make those initial contacts, you can't let them die by moving on to that next hot lead or the deal that came through. Your follow-up is just as important, if not more so, than that initial contact. A lot of people will make the call or have the meeting, get information, and then not put it all in a database. They soon forget about that person and never follow up. My team, I'll admit, has not been the best at following through, but if you can master this ability, your relationships and connections will be so much stronger. A relationship is not built with one call. And real estate, remember, is all about relationships.

Doing business with someone who called you once a few months ago is far less enticing than doing business with someone with whom you had lunch and who called or emailed you every two months since that initial meeting to check in.

A lot of brokers believe that an initial "no" is the end of the line for that contact. What's the point in following up with someone who has no interest in working with you and tells you so straight out?

Just recently, my lawyer referred me to a potential client. I emailed the prospect and he replied, saying his company had already moved down the road with another broker. I emailed back and said, "That's fine, but I would still love to meet with you. My friend says you're a great guy, and I always like meeting great guys."

He replied again negatively, saying he wasn't sure he could find the time. So I took the initiative and told him I would just stop by his office for ten minutes. And that's exactly what I did. I met him at his office, not with a sales pitch, but just to make that connection. By the end of my visit he was apologizing that he didn't have any work for me, but already naming several people he could refer me to. So one contact turned into several simply because I took the time and made the effort to meet someone in person.

If you approach these contacts with empathy and the goal to make a real human connection, rather than viewing them as a way to get more money, you will have mastered the art of chasing business. The cold call will feel and become a lot less chilly.

CHAPTER 29

A CLOSET OF OXXFORD SUITS

R. Craig Coppola

Around 1987, before we started Lee & Associates Arizona, I worked at Grubb & Ellis. I was three years into my career and just starting to make a bit of money. That year, I saw a *Time* magazine cover that read, "50 Things America Makes Better Than Anyone Else in the World."

I picked it up and started flipping through the list. One of the things on the list was an Oxxford suit. The article said that an Oxxford suit was the finest in the world, and if *Time* wrote it, in my eyes at the time, it had to be true.

Being the ambitious, young broker that I was, I said to myself, "One day I'm going to own an Oxxford suit." I set a goal to one day be able to afford a suit like that. I kept the article, and went about my day.

Later that year, I was closing business and knew I was going to have my best year yet. I decided to call Oxxford Clothes and find out what it takes to own one of its suits. I had no intention of buying one, but being a cold caller by nature I had no fear. My intent was to find out some information so I could calculate how long it would take me to get to a point where I could comfortably buy one.

I called the company's headquarters in Chicago, and said, "Hi, I'm Craig Coppola, I'm from Phoenix, Arizona, and I would like some more information to potentially buy a suit."

The woman on the other end said, "We don't actually sell them at this office; you have to buy them through retailers."

I asked which retailer Oxxford would recommend, and she gave me Maus & Hoffman, a high-end retailer based in Florida.

So I hung up and called Maus & Hoffman, and went through the whole thing again with its receptionist. "Hi, I'm Craig Coppola, I just called Oxxford headquarters and they said great things about you. I would like to potentially own a suit at some point, and wanted to get some more information."

The receptionist asked me to hold, and two seconds later, Bill Maus himself answered.

When he picked up, I instantly realized I was out of my league. I wasn't ready to buy the suit, and here I was talking to the company owner. But I couldn't hang up, so I gave him the same story, telling him I was just looking for some more information.

He stopped me. "Craig, where did you say you live again?"

"I'm out in Phoenix, Arizona."

"Great. I want you to give me your phone number, and then hang up, and I'm going to have someone give you a call in two minutes."

I had no idea what was going on, but at this point it was too late to back out. So I gave him my number, and sure enough two minutes later the phone rang.

"Hey, Craig, I just got off the phone with Bill Maus and I guess you want to buy an Oxxford suit. I'd like to get on your calendar sometime next week."

"What do you mean?" I asked him, a little apprehensive.

He said, "I live here in the Valley, and I want to get over and meet you. How does next Tuesday at 10 sound?"

Within five minutes of calling just for information, I had a meeting with someone in Arizona to discuss the suit. We set up our meeting and I hung up, wondering what in the world had just happened.

Tuesday at 10 rolled around and the receptionist called me at my desk. She said, "Craig, there's this really dapper, elderly man out here waiting to meet with you."

I walked into the lobby and there was this short, 70-year-old man, wearing the most incredible suit I'd ever seen. He was so finely dressed, with a pocket square and shined shoes, and he had a big trunk with him.

He handed me his card that read "Chief Designer for Oxxford Suits." I found out he had been in that position for 40 years. Ninety days earlier, he had retired to Sun City (in the Metro Phoenix area), and now did some occasional trunk shows. He was there to fit me for my suit.

What started as a call to one company in Chicago for information turned into a meeting with the former chief of design who had brought swatches and measuring tape with him to make me a suit. How do you say no to this 70-year-old man who had designed these suits for decades?

So I ordered a suit! Well, I didn't actually order a suit. I was in the middle of the river and the suit order was just happening. I didn't even know what it cost; I couldn't bring myself to ask. Three weeks later, he brought me this amazing suit and a bill for $1,800. (Back in the late '80s that was a lot of money. Still is today!)

The story does not end there. Every time he brought a suit to me to do final fittings, he rolled me into another suit. I ended up buying a number of suits over the next few years, building a relationship with this incredible man. For ten years, I was the best-dressed broker in Phoenix!

I make phone calls for information for a living. Some pan out and some don't. But when you know how to cold call, when you know the right things to say, you can get to anyone you want.

CHAPTER 30

"ME" TO "WE"

Bill Lee

Relationships with potential clients and with your competitors are vital to your success as a broker, but another relationship you can look to foster is a relationship with your peers within your own company, and more specifically, within your own team. Over the last thirty years, one of the biggest changes in commercial real estate has been the shift from working alone to working with team members all versed in different responsibilities. The brokers who are doing it all on their own with the help of just one assistant are becoming rare. Brokers are realizing that in our current environment it has become increasingly difficult to play the solo game. They need good people around them.

People who, for example, like to perform research and are good at it; people who like to work on contracts and effortlessly pull them together; entry-level people who serve as runners and are learning the business; assistants who schedule and manage projects; etc. A team offers you, the broker, the distinct advantage of support in your efforts to bring in deals and get them done while at the same time allowing you to do what you are uniquely good at.

Teaming up has also prompted a "me to we" shift; a change from looking out for yourself to looking at building relationships and leveraging the talents of others for the good of all. When you're out there, trying to win and make money to support your family, it's easy to get caught up in a "me" mentality. I know; I've been there. Many times, early in my career, I would ask myself, "What can I do, what should I be doing, to make myself more successful?" But a "we" mentality—in other words, a mindset focused on other people, a sharing approach, takes the focus off of the deal at hand and places it on the business plan. A plan designed for the long term, with integrated components, that is constantly in motion and not stopping for the efforts of the solo deal.

One of the best ways to refine your "we" mindset is to team up. When you bring together a group of strong, capable people with a common goal, then your mission and goals are amplified. A team forces you to look past how your success or failure impacts you, to how it can impact others, which can be extremely motivating.

Cultivating a "we" mindset intensifies everything we've discussed in this book so far. For example, competition. As any athlete can attest, competing as a team makes the competition much fiercer, because each team member wants to perform at his or her best so as to not let the team down, and so that together they can bring home a win.

You can even network as a team, utilizing your team members' contacts, or sharing your contacts with them when the need arises. That can deliver fast results because of the nearly instantaneous rapport that having a mutual connection can bring.

In addition, a "we" mentality nurtures a more sharing and giving heart, and as we've discussed, people with that kind of selflessness are people whom others respect and look up to. They are people everyone wants to work with.

Finally, building a team can take you to the next level of excellence within each step in the commercial real estate process. Teaming up opens doors that were previously closed to you. It allows you to expand your reach and multiply your value. And in the end, working as a team can be just plain fun!

One of the best teams I've ever seen—well, it has yet to be created! We've been talking hypothetical, right? The right team will beat the right individual; most of us will agree to that premise. But it is very difficult to build the right team; ask any team member. You need to match individual ability with individual motivation with individual discipline, and that is a tall order when you are bringing three to five, or more, people together on a team.

The easy part is determining individual strengths and subsequent value (compensation). The hard part is the intangible aspect of the various team members. If the lead dog (the rainmaker) is so talented that he or she brings in the business big time, then all else falls in line because the support team members always have their plate full. The rub then is how to keep that rainmaker happy with the value placed on the various team members.

Most teams (in my experience, 90 percent) fall apart in time. So, as great and productive as a team can be versus operating solo, much thought, preparation, and scrutiny need to happen when first putting the team members together.

When building a real estate team, take your cues from sports. For example, the San Antonio Spurs roster doesn't boast the most star-studded roster of celebrity players. There are incredibly talented players, like Tim Duncan and Tony Parker, but the team's success is based less on what these individual players do and more on how everyone works together as a team. They have team systems and processes in place that make them successful, leading them to huge wins. What really makes this team win however is a philosophy instilled by the coach and backed up by the GM and the owner. So a successful real estate team needs that same philosophy without the coach or owner to instill it, a very difficult situation because each member of the real estate team, if motivated, will grow in capability. The structure of that team needs to recognize this and provide compensation for it or turnover will happen.

On a real estate team, you want your superstar players, but you also want each player to be able to work with everyone else. You want to avoid having anyone on your team who is looking out only for him or herself, who has to be the star at the expense of everyone else. Bring in people who can support each team member and adopt the team goal as their own.

Part of building those successful team systems is recognizing each team member's strengths and weaknesses. When you have a post player, you don't have him shooting 3-pointers, right? Let team members perform the tasks where they will shine. Being successful in a team, however, is as much about recognizing what you can't do as it is celebrating what you can do.

My wife has a saying: "I can't go there." When she doesn't connect with something, she says, "I just can't go there; it's painful for me." She is so in touch with who she is and how she can function that she knows she can't do certain things and go certain places, physically and emotionally. Instead of wasting her time and creating anxiety for herself, she recognizes her limitations and respects them.

Instead of viewing this as weakness, consider this ability to recognize your limitations as a virtue. Once you acknowledge those places and activities where you won't have success, you can focus on the things and the places where you can shine. This will save you so much time, energy, and headaches. It will for your team, too.

And that's the beauty of a team. Others can fill in those gaps and do those things you can't do. So find team members who are different from you, who love and can do the things you don't want to do, better than you ever could. Through your team, once again, you enhance your value. You stop wasting time trying to be productive in an area where it will never happen, and let someone else take on that responsibility. You increase your value by increasing what you can offer and enhancing your efficiency, and that's what a team is all about.

In short, being on a team lets you do what you do best most of the time, creating more fun, greater productivity, and less anxiety! And what is the value of less anxiety in your life? Think about that the next time you review the compensation plan for your team.

CHAPTER 31

THE LONE RANGER
IS DEAD

R. Craig Coppola

I'm going to go out on a limb and say, if you are a lone ranger, you are a dying breed. I used to be one of those, but a few years ago, I saw the light, built a team, and never looked back.

The decision to team up wasn't an easy one. I thought, "That means I'm going to have to manage people. It means I'm going to have to figure out compensation arrangements. It means doing a lot of stuff that a) I don't particularly like to do, and b) will distract me from finding and closing deals, which is the stuff I love to do." The one thing that kept the idea of a team on my radar was I do like teaching and mentoring.

I didn't get serious about pulling together a team until several years after I started working with Dan Sullivan, creator of The Strategic Coach® Program. He is a remarkable guy, a true mentor to me. Dan is the one who showed me how I could take my abilities further, leverage myself, and get to a much higher level in my career. He told me I could not do it alone and then showed me how to think about a team.

Before Dan's concept, the thought of building a team seemed abstract to me. It wasn't like the world of commercial real estate where the deal points are negotiated and then all spelled out in the contract. I liked systems, but managing people to me didn't feel very systematic. But then Dan introduced me to the unique ability. With that, the idea of a team made sense; it seemed attainable.

There are the four levels of competency:

1. Incompetence—no matter how much you try and work at it, you will never be good at it.

2. Competence—you work really hard for a long period of time but you still are just okay.

3. Excellence—people tell you that you are good at something, others give you props for your talents.

4. Unique Ability—excellence plus passion; something you do well that you also have passion for. The key to unique ability is having both. You can't just have passion for painting. If you don't have the skill, it is just a hobby. You also can't just be excellent at writing; if you don't love it, you won't pursue it.

Understanding where you fall on these four levels, in all different areas of life, allows you to understand better your strengths and weaknesses, your likes and dislikes.

This knowledge, for me, was the first step to building a strong team. For years I worked on refining my own unique abilities, honing them and practicing them. But still I was stuck. I would start projects and find no way to finish them. I understood my weaknesses, but no matter how hard I tried, I remained incompetent or merely competent at key things.

Over the years, I've discovered that one of my unique abilities is conceiving ideas. My process includes having an idea and "dumping" it, meaning I write it down and even include a bunch of research and detailed plans on what it would look like. But then those ideas used to just sit there for years, with no further progress. I had actually created a black hole list.

That was the list where ideas and projects would go to die. I was so frustrated, because I had these great ideas but none of them would ever get anywhere.

From that frustration and the understanding of the unique ability became the inspiration to build my team. I stopped seeing a team as people I had to manage and started seeing them as people who could take my ideas and, step-by-step, bring them to life.

On my real estate team, everyone has a role. For example, Chelsea and Erica are my follow-throughs. Their unique ability is to take ideas and follow through on them, planning the step-by-step process to execute each idea. Having them on my team has allowed our output to increase tenfold. Now, when we start projects, we actually finish them.

An example of how this works is my weekly emails. Every week I send out a narrative, interesting article, video, or graph about some hot topic in the industry. I've recently added a personal weekly narrative that follows the rules laid out in my book, *The Fantastic Life*. My unique ability is finding these interesting articles and writing a few thoughts so readers can quickly digest the article's relevance.

Chelsea and Erica, my follow-throughs, take control and format my emails, and then send them on to my daughter, Kellie. Kellie's unique ability is writing and editing. She has a passion for it, and she takes the few quick lines I've put down and rewrites them, edits them, and makes sure they are clean and coherent. Chelsea and Erica keep these emails organized and send them out to over 50,000 people each week.

This short process is just one example of how my team operates in all our transactions. Internally, with our organization and the systems we have in place, we are able to thrive. Each member plays a key role in our operations, and playing off each one's unique strengths allows us to be a top-producing team year after year.

Once you understand your own unique abilities and your own weak areas, you can find others with unique abilities that fill the gaps, so as a team you overcome every weakness. Instead of wasting valuable time trying to improve yourself in an area you will never master or have no passion for, consider finding others who live for that kind of work, do these jobs well, and can do them for you.

It's like plumbing. I am no handyman. I won't even pretend to know what goes on under the sink. But I have a great plumber on stand-by in case something goes wrong at the house. I could spend hundreds of dollars at a hardware store and hours online trying to learn how to fix a clogged drain, but that would be a waste of my time. Instead, I call a plumber who can easily fix it because that's his talent. The plumber is on my team.

It takes years to discover and refine your unique abilities. Your unique abilities can grow and even change as you learn more and practice those things you were competent or excellent at. Your unique ability combined with your team members' unique abilities allows you to expand your value.

If you're not sure what your unique abilities are, talk to others who know you well to see what they think you are truly excellent at. Identify just a few abilities. Then learn how to build on your abilities and apply it to all you do. Don't worry about what you're not good at. Bring in others to compensate for your weaknesses. Learn how to fill the gaps in teams, and utilize your ability to add value wherever you go. Then it's "Hi-ho Silver, away!" for good.

CHAPTER 32

GET OUT
THE FILTER

Bill Lee

Like Craig, making the decision to build a team wasn't easy for me. And it led to one of the hardest lessons I've learned in my career: the importance of filtering out people who aren't adding value to my life or my business. As brokers, we boast independence and self-sufficiency. But it doesn't take long in the business before you realize that the people around you have a much bigger impact on your success than you thought they would. It's next to impossible to be a one-person act. There just aren't enough hours in the day.

That means every broker and every manager has to learn how to hire and how to fire. If you can't build a team that functions well and delivers results, you won't get very far. So understanding how to bring in good people to work with you is vital to your business's success. Equally important is knowing when to make a change and let go of the people who do not live up to your expectations. None of this people stuff is easy, but it is necessary if you're committed to excellence and being your best, and creating a working environment that is good for everyone.

I have to admit, I am not always good at following my own advice. I tend to build relationships with many people whom I like, but who are really in the wrong profession. I find it hard to tell them that, and while eventually they find it out for themselves, they waste a lot of time in the process. So I've had to learn the hard way to deal with these people head on.

What you need is something I call a filter to separate the right people from the, well, let's say not right. So what's the filter look like? This one doesn't reside in your sink; it can't sit on your desk, or on your computer screen, or in an app on your iPad. This filter is a list of viable measurements that will help you filter out the people who you don't believe will be successful in your business or within your organization. Maybe you want to avoid people who have a negative attitude, or a lazy work ethic. Maybe you want to strain out people who are more concerned about themselves than the success of the team. Whatever the characteristics you want to avoid, you have to have a system in place in your company to strain them out.

To me, the best place to start building your system is with your values. Companies often list their values on their website, not only to let their clients know what they stand for but also to let potential employees know what they are getting into if they want to work there. Workers whose beliefs do not align with those of the company are often filtered out when they go to the website. If they feel they might have trouble living up to those values, it may be enough to stop them from applying and wasting their time and yours. This is the ideal situation, but it means your values have to be well-thought-out and truly meaningful to your organization.

When Lee & Associates opened its first office, I reached out to several acquaintances and peers to give them the opportunity to join. We had a great structure in place for a partnership (eventually a corporation) with shared profits and equal voice. We laid the foundation to open new offices and provide brokers the chance to make huge returns on their own initiative.

I believe whole-heartedly in this unique business structure, and in its accompanying mission and goals. I was so excited about what we were doing that I could barely restrain myself from talking about it with other people. I believed that they would be just as interested as I was; after all, an opportunity like this doesn't come around every day. In fact, there was no company like Lee & Associates before it, and there hasn't been one set up like us since (we will discuss why later in this book).

In those early days I pitched a lot of people to come join our company. One person I sat down with was a colleague of mine in the business named Pete. Pete worked for CBRE, a large regional company at the time and the largest in the industry today. A good company that I respect very much.

I took Pete to lunch one day and pitched him on the company. I told him about our structure and gave him the chance to become a partner, a part owner. This was the proverbial ground-floor opportunity. He was very courteous and listened to my dialogue, never once interrupting.

When I finished talking, he said, "Well, Bill, here's the thing. Your guys don't make as much money as the guys in my office. And you don't have much institutional product. Beyond that, you don't have a deep bench. So I can't really think of why I'd like to go to work for you."

He laid me out, and his words hit hard. I couldn't believe that he didn't see how unique and valuable this opportunity was for him. My confidence was set back, and I wondered how many others would feel the same way.

It took me a couple of days to get back my "giddy up" and realize we might be better off not having him join us. Pete appreciated what CBRE had to offer. It was a big, visible company with a name brand that gave him credibility. Having that company on his business card allowed him to walk into any office with confidence that he would be received in the manner in which he desired.

The name Lee & Associates in those early days meant nothing. It carried no credibility. But what we did provide was opportunity. We offered brokers who believed in themselves the chance to take home significantly more of the money that they earned, have a voice in the decisions that their office made, and be able to invest in the growth of the company. They would have to bring in the business on their own, but if they were confident in their abilities, their success would be rewarded much higher than working for any of our competitors.

I always believed that I had more opportunities on my plate to work on than I had time to do it, so why wouldn't I want to work for a company that let me keep the lion's share of my commissions?

And that experience led to our first filter: our future salespeople had to be confident in their own abilities. If they desired a big brand name behind them, this opportunity, this new entity, wasn't for them. As we continued to develop our company, other filters emerged, but this one was big.

We've had many individuals like Pete who either didn't join us initially or left because they didn't understand where we were going. They didn't share our values. And they didn't have what it took to get to the goal. They valued the big brand more than they valued the potential returns they could make with us. We began to learn in those very early days that if people needed the brand to feel confident, they wouldn't work out.

And there's nothing wrong with that. Brokers like Pete like the corporate structure, and the brand of a national brokerage behind them. Pete was successful in a company that offered those things to him. It doesn't mean one way was right and the other wrong, it was about what was right for him and what was right for us.

At Lee & Associates, our partnership structure is our filter. A whole set of values comes with it—a culture and a purpose. We are what we are. Even as we grew into a national brand, we didn't change our focus or values to appeal to everyone. Rather, we held true to our beliefs, and in doing so created something special.

Every company should have a filter, a set of values or goals that it uses to weed out the people who don't fit. If you stay true to yourself and your mission, you will attract the kind of people who believe as you do, who will help you grow and achieve your dreams. Find people who value what you value and strain out the rest.

This lesson applies to the people you surround yourself with at home too. One of the biggest roadblocks on the path to excellence is the people in your life. Many times, your friends and family might not understand the path you're embarking on. They might judge you, criticize you, and predict your failure. They might smile and nod when you talk about your goals, but inwardly express their disbelief in you ever achieving them.

When you surround yourself with people who doubt you, how long can you motivate yourself to keep going? But when you spend time with people who lift you up, who believe in you and support you, you'll find it much easier to reach your goals.

So get out your filter and weed out the people who aren't a positive influence, who don't align with your values or goals. Learn to filter out others' negativity, and surround yourself with people whose positivity far exceeds any doubt.

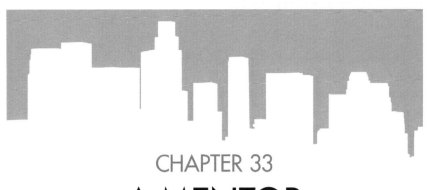

CHAPTER 33

A MENTOR
IN DISGUISE

Bill Lee

You never know who is going to be influential in your life. You just never know. It might be that loud talker you find so annoying, but who seems to get more home runs than anyone else, or it could be the new guy you just met. My point is, be open. He or she could be a mentor in disguise.

When I worked at Grubb & Ellis, my cubicle was next to John Sutherland's. John had only two years of real estate experience when I started, but that seemed like a lot to a guy who had no experience. So I watched and listened to him. He was an incredibly serious broker. He was all work from the moment he stepped into the office to the minute he left every night. He never engaged in bar talk and he didn't socialize in the coffee room. He was always focused on the deal.

John was there to get it done. That isn't to say he was all work and no play. John had a very active family life; he was married with two daughters, and he was very involved in their sports and activities. He had his interests and hobbies outside the office also, but his personal life never mixed with his business life. Once in the office, he was focused, and that was that.

John had a booming voice that almost everyone could hear from anywhere in the office. He had that kind of voice that carried, and all his phone calls and conversations drifted through the paper-thin cubicle walls to where I sat. I'd be lying if I said it didn't bug me at times. Still, during the early years, I listened to him make deals and argue with landlords, always respecting his methods but never taking the time to ask him questions or try to learn directly from him.

I realized, too late in fact, that John was one of the greatest mentors I ever had. He was a person I really looked up to and admired. He had drive, dedication, and complete focus. Because we worked together, side by side as peers, it never crossed my mind to consider him a mentor. Mentors are supposed to be older and wiser, right? But that's exactly what he was. He motivated me, without either of us realizing it, to work harder and stay focused. I wanted to make the kinds of deals he made and demonstrate the same kind of dedication that he demonstrated. I wanted to win the way he won, and deal with failure the way he dealt with it. I found myself almost subconsciously mirroring him, and learning from him.

John has since passed away, and I never got the chance to thank him for his mentorship. I sometimes wonder how much more I could have learned from him if I had taken the time to ask him questions directly, rather than just passively observing his success. If I had recognized him as the mentor he was, I might have had more chances to grow at an earlier stage in my career. I might have gotten farther faster.

You can find mentors by seeking out people whom you see as successful, and then watch, listen, and learn how they conduct their business. Be observant, listen to your gut, and you will soon realize how others are motivating you inside and outside of your office. You can find inspiration in the people around you who work with excellence to be the best they can be.

I discovered another mentor much earlier on, when I was still in high school. I attended an all-boys Catholic High School of approximately 300 students. In an environment like that, you get pretty close with your classmates. With no girls, and coaches and teachers who want you to play every sport and participate in every extra-curricular activity, you bond very quickly.

I still speak regularly with about ten of my high school classmates. I've remained very close with one in particular, Henry Burdick. Henry transferred into the school as a junior, having attended other boarding schools before. He was born in Cuba and had a very gregarious personality. You couldn't help but like him. Henry and I became very close: classmates, teammates, college roommates, best man at each other's weddings, investment partners, and lifelong friends. He was always a step ahead of me on the maturity scale, having experienced living away from home at an early age while attending boarding schools. He was also just blessed with an incredible personality and an amazing presence.

I remember in high school that while I, and the rest of our pals, were caught up in the typical high school "nothingness," Henry would verbalize his desire to become a millionaire. A few years later, when he was just out of college and newly married, Henry didn't waste much time. He started selling vitamins to pharmacies and then teamed up with a pharmacist to start his own company. Today, that company is one of the largest in the industry with sales over a billion dollars. You might recognize their brand name: Nature Made.

Around the time Henry started his company, I was just entering the commercial real estate industry. We would talk most nights about the trials and tribulations he encountered getting his company started and it was very interesting for me. You know how some of your friends like to talk and others like to listen? Well, that's how it went between the two of us during those conversations—he talked, I listened. What I didn't realize at the time was that Henry was mentoring me for the day I would start my own company. I learned about the daily motions of a new business startup, and when the day came to start Lee & Associates, I had no fear as I had already been exposed to the start-up experience through my friend and mentor.

Just like I had John Sutherland and Henry Burdick as mentors and didn't really know it, you might already have a mentor in your life and be completely unaware, too. Take the time to consider the relationships you have with other people. Is there someone you greatly admire, someone whose actions or values you would like to emulate?

Don't wait until it's too late to recognize the people in your life who inspire you. They don't have to be perfect, they don't have to be older, and they don't have to be your superior. I don't have many regrets, but John deserved to know the impact he had on me and still has on me to this day. But I never gave him that chance.

Call up those people who are impacting your life, and take them to lunch now. Share with them the impact they are having on you. Ask them questions. Be proactive in building the kinds of relationships that will help you grow and help you find your own excellence.

Now, having said that, how many can you think of? My guess is that there are not many, and that's too bad. All the more reason to let that person or people know the impact they have had, or are having, on you today. As for Henry, I look forward to sending him this book. I'm sure if I told him these things, he would think I'm playing some kind of joke on him. You know how good friends can be.

CHAPTER 34

HOW ABOUT A DOSE OF WISDOM WITH THAT ROOT CANAL?

R. Craig Coppola

When I first moved to Phoenix, there were a few things I had to do in order to get settled. Items at the top of the list were move into a house, get set up at a new job, and find a dentist. Being particular about my dentists, I did some research and went to a few different dentists around town until I found one I liked.

My dentist of choice was Jim McDonald, and he had a practice only a few minutes from my house. One of his high school classmates was Bill Gosnell, one of the top brokers in the U.S. (and one of my future partners who helped start Lee & Associates Arizona), so with me being in commercial real estate, we had an instant connection. After the hygienist cleaned my teeth, we sat down and talked for a while and I really enjoyed our first conversation. He was smart and interesting, and it was by far one of the best dental appointments I'd ever had.

So I started going to Jim's practice, and made it a point to book the last appointment of the day anytime I went. The hygienist would clean my teeth, and afterward, when the office was closed, Jim and I would sit around and talk.

Through these talks Jim became a mentor. We talked about everything from business to family to travel. A man on a completely different business track, with a different kind of career success, almost two decades older than me, quickly became one of my greatest friends and role models. For almost thirty years now, three to four times a year, I still make the last appointment with Jim and we have long talks afterward.

I'll give you an example of the kind of conversations we have. This past year, he told me he's come to recognize that some things in his life have a shelf life. For example, Jim is a heli-skier. For twenty years, he went to Whistler, a skiing mecca in the Canadian Rockies, to heli-ski every Christmas. For the first four or five years, it was fantastic. The next four or five years it was good. The last ten years, he was doing it just because he thought he should.

For Jim, heli-skiing had a shelf life. After a few years it had lost its value. Last year he chose to stay home for Christmas and didn't miss the skiing at all. Instead, he put his focus on new activities that made him happy.

Now he looks at everything he does in regard to its shelf life and whether or not it still adds value to his life. Through his story, I've been inspired to do the same and remove the things from my life that are past their expiration date.

This is just a sample of the kinds of conversations I have with my dentist, my friend, and my mentor. In terms of just learning from someone about life, my dentist has taught me more than most of my other mentors.

Mentors don't have to be someone within your business, or even someone you see every day. Mentors are people who have a tremendous impact on your life. They are people you enjoy talking to and learning from; people who give more than they get.

Bill Lee is another important mentor to me, but in a different way. I enjoy speaking with Bill, hearing about his life after retirement, for many reasons. Bill is a friend, but he's a great example whom I look up to when picturing my life in twenty years. He's retired but still competing. He has the time to pursue his passions, connect with his family, and find ways to occupy his time since leaving the business. If I could retire half as gracefully as Bill, I would be pretty content.

Finding someone like Bill, someone who is going or has gone through an experience that lies ahead, helps you envision where you are going or where you would like to go. Talking with someone like Jim the dentist, with different life experiences and perspective, is just as beneficial. These kinds of relationships open your eyes to the world around you, and provide perspective on the path to excellence. They are worth finding and fostering. But here's a hint: be open and they will find you.

CHAPTER 35

AL, THE MENTOR OF ALL MENTORS

Bill Lee

You can have mentors at all stages of your life, but eventually, having gained enough knowledge and experience, the day comes when you may become a mentor yourself. You reach a point when it is time to pass along your own wisdom. Like John Sutherland, Henry Burdick, and Jim McDonald, you might already be a mentor to someone without realizing it. Or, like my friend Al Fabiano, you might be actively seeking out people you can guide and teach.

Al, now retired, loved to mentor and teach young brokers. Even when he was active in the sales profession, he found no greater joy than nurturing others and helping them grow and succeed. As hard as it is to believe in our business, Al did not find the same fulfillment in closing a million-dollar deal himself (although, of course, his wife did). His true passion lies in leading others to closing those deals and more.

When Al was managing our Riverside Lee & Associates office, he mentored the twenty-five-plus people who worked there. They would line up outside his doors every day waiting to talk with him, get his advice, celebrate wins, and regain their confidence after failures. A colleague once commented, "Al should make everyone take numbers like at a butcher's shop. That way everyone would have a chance to talk with him."

Al is one of the best mentors I know for two reasons: He knows how to listen and he knows how to empathize. He's no softie, but you might say he has a caring personality, and he genuinely likes listening to people talk about their problems and fears. He is also able to put himself in other people's shoes and feel their anxieties. Because of these talents, he can communicate with people more effectively, and offer them individualized advice to help them overcome their weaknesses.

I've learned over the years that we all want to be heard. And for that reason, we gravitate toward people who genuinely listen and care about us. That means listening is everything. Another skill of a great mentor is offering advice in a way that doesn't sound preachy or all-knowing.

If I sound like Al's biggest fan, I might be. But he has plenty of other big fans to go around. The way he shares his wisdom is just magical. He has a way of telling people what they need to do in a particular situation, and they don't even realize he's told them. People arrive at their own conclusions, so they are inclined to act on them. This is a rare and valuable mentoring skill that you can learn and share with others. Listen, empathize, then talk if necessary.

One of Al's greatest success stories involved a broker in the office who didn't think he had what it took to get the big deals. He came to Al just about ready to quit because he didn't believe he would ever be successful. Al encouraged him to stay on his path, keep working hard, and stay motivated. He told him to take advantage of the growth market and build a future by networking feeder market brokers. A few years later, that same broker was achieving multiple million-dollar deals every year (and is quoted in another chapter in this book).

Sometimes it just takes someone believing in us to bring out our potential. Many times, we just need someone to tell us that we can do it—we can push through our fears and insecurities and achieve our dreams. Most people have the ability to be successful; we just need a little mentoring. We all need it. And as you are sitting reading this, you may be able to provide it.

Al is retired now. If there was a Lee & Associates Hall of Fame, Al would be in it. Not for closing the most deals, but for everything he did for everyone else. And he's still doing it. The fact is, once you become a mentor, you likely will always be a mentor. Your impact will be massive and live far beyond your lifetime. Not bad for just listening, for just caring. Oh, and did I mention, the Riverside Lee & Associates office has always been one of the top five offices in the Lee organization for the past 20 years? Wonder who was behind that?

CHAPTER 36

KNOW THE 'V' WORD AND WORSHIP IT DAILY

Bill Lee

When brainstorming the title and overarching theme of this book, I settled on the word "excellence" to describe the brokers I perceived as going above and beyond the average professional, the ones who truly stuck out above the crowd. But I just as easily could have called this process "adding value" because that's what excellent brokers do—they bring value all the time.

The true key to excellence is knowing how to add value, and there are many different ways we do this. Value can be having a strong understanding of the market, having enough significant experience that you can see things the way they will be rather than as they are, having an efficient team that can provide a more diverse value package, having an excellent referral base, having youthful energy—the possibilities are endless. Value is what you bring to the table that makes you stand out and that will work in the client's favor. It's your sales pitch to every potential client.

Getting the kind of business you want means you have to be able to translate that value and convey it to your client. You have to show each client how the value you bring will work to his or her advantage. And the trick is, you have to do it in such a way that you outshine your competition. In other words, when you can bring more value to a client than your competitor can, you win. Is the competitor in you getting excited yet?

One great example of value is Jim Snyder. My God, this fifty-plus still looks like he is twenty-five. I think he discovered a tattoo parlor in Newport Beach, where he works in the Lee office, and had a permanent smile embedded on his face. You cannot not like Jim. He listens, he looks you in the eye, he smiles when he talks. He is engaging, and he makes you feel like you are his best friend. Then, he slays you with his value. He knows his market like no other. He knows everything about everything in the area he works. He uses his personality to open doors and then, like a precision surgeon, he does everything right to build and maintain relationships. He has been the top salesman in his office for over twenty years.

Where and how did he develop this value? As a freshman in high school, he stood at 5'3" and was too small to play football and basketball, his favorite sports. He thought he would try tennis, but had never played the sport before. So he bought a tennis racket and went to the local tennis club to watch the participants. He asked an instructor to teach him the basics and paid out of his own pocket for the lessons with money earned from a part time job.

He got so good, so fast, that he made the varsity team as a freshman and became league champion his last three years in high school. His senior year he played in AAU tournaments across the country and gained such notoriety that he received a scholarship to the University of California Irvine and immediately became their number one player. He turned professional immediately after graduation, winning against many name professionals.

He eventually realized, however, that rising to the top in the tennis profession was not in the cards for him. As he searched for a career he wandered into the Lee & Associates Newport Beach office in 1984 and has never looked back since. Jim will write his own book some day and I'll read it cover to cover. Jim gets it done in his own way. He uses his personality, discipline, and knowledge to bring value, all the time.

The problem is, everyone says they offer value. Of course they do, everyone is trying to sell themselves. Often you'll find your competition using the same buzzwords you do to convey their value. But sometimes they don't actually possess the ability to deliver that value. Sometimes they're just words.

There's nothing more frustrating than losing a deal to a team who says they are "experienced" when you have ten years on them. The client can't always tell who actually has value and who is bluffing. That's why you have to not only tell the client about the value you bring, but also be able to tangibly demonstrate that value in a way that makes sense to that client specifically.

How do you do that? I'll tell you a story.

Some years back I did a build-to-suit with Timberland. This was a big transaction, about 425,000 square feet, and it was a competition. Timberland was working with CBRE at the time, so I had to compete to get the business.

I got to Timberland through one of its board members, who was also a board member for Circuit City, a company I'd done business with before. He got me in touch with the right guy in charge of the deal, who agreed to give me a shot at the business.

They needed a build-to-suit within a year, in a specific free trade zone. I immediately went to Ontario, California, and started doing my research for the right site. I knew this deal wasn't just about finding a location; if I wanted to beat out the competition, I had to demonstrate that my value-add was greater than the other guy's.

As part of my preparation, I utilized the storyboarding method I had learned years before to organize all the different parts of the project. I made sure I knew who the most competitive contractors were and their most experienced job superintendent. I knew the best architects and their best draftsman. I also found the best civil engineer with the most experience in that specific market. I made sure I knew what the entitlement issues were and their related timelines. I requested final cost estimations from each vendor, and calculated all the totals.

I had all this done even prior to getting involved in the Timberland transaction. Having this research was my competitive edge. When the Timberland guy came to town, I knew it was time to use it.

I showed the Timberland representative the location, and then sat him down with the top contractor, architect, and civil engineer in the area, all of whom I had prior relationships with. These vendors all knew what my specific focus was; they'd seen my story room and had contributed to it and they knew I was working in my wheelhouse. I wasn't just the broker in the conversation playing the supporting role. I was the leader of the meeting and the conversation that took place in it.

My client saw me in that role with these experts who had unparalleled resumes that fit the build-to-suit's needs perfectly. He saw that they were the support people to me, rather than the other way around. I was not only telling him I could bring value, I was handing him tangible examples of that value on a platter!

My client saw that he would get value from me by being set up with the right vendors. I had even gone so far as to invite the right drafter for the architect, and the right superintendent for the contractor to demonstrate how we could move the timeline along. I had put together an entire team that would be dedicated to this project, and Timberland wouldn't have to do a thing.

In addition, I gave him a sheet of paper detailing everything he could expect in regard to cost. I knew the shell cost of the building, the construction costs for add ons, the architecture cost, the engineering costs, all the various tenant improvement costs, entitlement costs and their respective timelines. I had totaled everything up to get a final number, and then factored in the various lease rate options, whether they would finance it or not, and included those yields as well.

Because I had researched these costs ahead of time with the vendors, when Timberland got the bids back they matched my numbers perfectly. The vendors couldn't manipulate the costs or take advantage of the situation, because they had already given the numbers.

That's value. That's adding value on an up-front basis. My client knew walking out of that meeting exactly what he would get from me. It was more than just a building; it was an entire team of professionals, a fixed final cost, and confidence that this job would be done correctly and on time.

Who do you think won that deal?

Excellence is going above and beyond the average crowd, and knowing how to translate that value to your potential clients. Learn how to demonstrate your value, whatever it may be. Here are a few questions to get you started:

What makes me different from the competition?

What am I most proud of in regard to my career?

What do I lack and how can I compensate for it?

What about me stands out in this market/time?

How can my skills work in favor of the client?

How can I demonstrate this value in a tangible way?

What knowledge do I have that my competitors don't?

CHAPTER 37

YOUNG AND INEXPERIENCED

Bill Lee

Are you young and inexperienced? Did you know that those attributes might be an advantage in this world of commercial real estate?

This is what the world of experienced client investors most likely thinks about you:

- You probably don't have much to do other than make cold calls.

- You probably don't have many "preferred" investor relationships, if any.

- You probably don't have a very good understanding of pricing.

- You probably can be manipulated by an experienced investor.

You might look at those ideas as negative, but think about it. Why wouldn't an experienced investor want to do business with you if he thinks you are apt to come up with something first, before his "busy" regular broker finds out about your recently uncovered opportunity? Then the investor is not put in a competitive situation with other interested investors. The opportunity exists to make a good value purchase with you.

That could be the case, but investors are waiting for you to "make the case." So understand this and make calls all day, every day, until you find a buyer. In every call, make sure that you let that investor know that you can be a good resource in the future because of a plethora of reasons they might not have considered before.

Once you've made the initial contact, the following should help you follow through:

- Arrange a meeting with the investor.

- At the meeting, get to know his or her investment criteria.

- Ask the investor for an opportunity to do business with him or her, looking for a specific investment to purchase or a listing to sell or lease.

- Look the investor right in the eye and tell him, or her, the following with complete sincerity: "I am committed and determined to achieve at the highest level of commercial real estate sales. I will pay whatever price is necessary to accomplish this. I have very few established relationships at this time, so I will *never forget* those who help me get started. I will always show them my deals first and make them aware of other deals in my office as soon as I become aware of them. This is my promise. Can you help me get started on this path now?"

How do I know that this will work? Because it worked for me.

I opened the City of Industry office in late 1989, and we had very few listings in the San Gabriel Valley, Mid-Cities, and Vernon/Commerce market at that time. CBRE, C&W, and Seeley (now Colliers) all had very successful offices in this marketplace. I had very limited knowledge of this market, having come up from Orange County, and all my clients knew I lacked experience here.

I identified the larger landlord entities, desperate to get some listings to gain some traction and help recruit and give the office presence. I struck out with Majestic (the largest landlord brokered most of its own business). I struck out with Mapes (a very active developer doing most of its business with Colliers). I struck out with Prudential (the dealmaker needed to justify his broker decisions to upper management).

Then I made a pitch to O'Donnell (an active local developer doing business with CBRE and Colliers). I told the dealmaker, JR Wetzel, that I would never forget the first developer who helped me get started in the new market, and that I would make sure our agents did not either. We got the listing.

I then talked my way into a presentation to AT&T who was making a change on a 600,000 square foot listing in the Commerce market. We had almost no history in that market, few listings, little reputation, etc. but I knew the dealmaker was upset with his previous relationship because, among other things, that the broker was not in regular communication with him about the status of the property. (A big lesson…it's one thing if nothing is happening on a listing, but it's another if you are not communicating to your client regularly). I walked into the presentation against all our major competitors and told the client that, among other things, I would provide him a list of what I was going to do to market his building at the first of every week, and a summary of what I did at the end of every week. I hit his hot button and got that listing.

And suddenly, our new office had some momentum. We canvassed those listings, and within ten years we became the number-one office in those markets, a title we retain today.

The point is, you don't have to be the number-one choice if you can bring a client long-term value. When you are young or can be viewed negatively for some other reason, reach into your mind and determine what value you can bring to the client beyond the obvious where you might not make the cut.

CHAPTER 38

THE ART OF REFINEMENT

R. Craig Coppola

Once you've made some progress on your path to excellence, and you start seeing the fruits of your labors in the deals you land or the awards you accrue, it's easy to get complacent. I've seen several brokers hit the ground running in the first decade of their career, only to slowly hit a ceiling. They find a formula of success that works for them, and never take the time to reevaluate, grow, or change.

Truly excellent brokers aren't content with staying in one place too long. They never rest on their laurels, but rather keep refining their processes, always seeking how they can be better, faster, and smarter. As we've stated in this book several times, the pursuit of excellence is much more about the journey than it is the end destination.

For many years, I wanted to get business from New York based companies. New York was and is the place for corporate headquarters, and if I wanted to get business from a large company, that was the place to get it. So every year I cold-called companies in New York, telling them I would be there a certain day, and set up meetings with them.

It took me a while to get a formula in place, but eventually I had it down. For ten years in a row, I would get on the red eye flight, arrive in New York at 7:00 a.m., shave and change in the airport bathroom, and have five meetings set up for the day. I would bring five dozen bags of fresh tortillas from my favorite Mexican food restaurant in Phoenix, and I would carry a bag into each meeting I had that day. I would have meetings all day long, then rush to the airport and get on the last flight home. I'd be back home that night and go to work the next day.

A lot of brokers would hear a story like that and think I was crazy. Who in his right mind would spend twenty-four hours traveling and meeting with these companies, just on the off chance that they might be interested in working with him? But those are the kinds of things excellent brokers do that average brokers would never bother themselves with. I had plenty of opportunities I could have chased in Phoenix, in my home market, but I wanted more. I wanted new clients, different deals, bigger transactions. Even after I accrued quite a bit of success in the Phoenix market, I never stopped chasing those national deals.

We have to do what we need to do, every day, learning to break through our comfort zones and try new things to achieve excellence. The best brokers I know have years of experience, but they don't have the same year of experience over and over again. Each year is different—different clients, deal types, markets, etc. They don't just do a thousand agency transactions, they do renewals and tenant leasing and national accounts. They grow every year and refine their process, seeking new ways to improve.

Those chasing excellence don't say, "I made this million-dollar deal so now I'm done." They start looking for bigger deals, different clients, and other transactions outside of their comfort zone. They perfect their processes until—well, there is no "until." They never stop growing and learning and refining.

When I was a runner at the beginning of my career, I ran for a fabulous broker named Ron. He had fifteen to twenty years of experience, but he never did anything differently. So he had a cap, a ceiling, on his income. He had an incredibly successful career, but he could never break through to that next level. He was stuck.

Don't be content to be merely good. Or even great. Continue striving. Don't lose momentum because you've accrued success. There is always a way to improve.

Here is a suggestion: each quarter, review your TIP (Transactions in Progress) to see what types of deals you are working.

Is there:

1. At least one transaction that will make you $500,000? How about $1,000,000?

2. At least one transaction outside your normal market or submarket?

3. A type of deal you have not worked before (a sale, a consulting assignment, etc.)?

If not, start chasing down leads in each area until you have a varied and, yes, slightly intimidating array of business.

CHAPTER 39

GET OUT YOUR
CRYSTAL BALL

Bill Lee

I love basketball, and one thing I often think about is how much basketball players have improved over the years. The skill levels of today's 8th graders, high schoolers, college athletes, and professionals are vastly different from what they were more than a decade ago. The last 8th grade teams I coached would have destroyed the first 8th grade teams I coached. And it wasn't because I'm a better coach now than I was then. Kids today just *are* really good. The high school and college teams of today would demolish teams their same level a decade ago. Each year, the sport improves, finding new and innovative ways to take the game to the next level.

I draw the same connection to commercial real estate practitioners, marveling at how much more impressive the deals they put together today are compared to the work they did twenty years ago. Brokers today accomplish far more than they did when I first started in the business. As in basketball, industry always finds new ways to evolve and grow.

The question then becomes, how can you apply that knowledge to help you gain an edge? If you could incorporate just some of tomorrow's changes today, think how far ahead you would be compared to your associates who are still trying to master, or maybe are still in denial of, last year's change. It doesn't matter which business you are in, but it is particularly important in commercial real estate. Opening your eyes to the changes taking place right now in terms of technology, our society, and our nation will do more to set you up for future excellence than almost anything else.

There's nothing more dangerous than remaining stuck in the past, and many brokers spend their time reliving old glories or failures, or can't move out of the present. They are still trapped recovering from the recession of 2008 and so can't see the fluctuations in the market that are about to hit. Very few can look past this moment, past this deal, past this upcoming weekend, to make a strategic, long-term plan for the future.

The CRE business changes dramatically at times such that brokers who create a vision of the future that they believe in and can demonstrate with facts, are the ones who always seem to find themselves ahead of the pack. In so doing they enhance their reputation as a reliable consultant. And once you are considered a consultant as well as a broker, you have put yourself in the cat bird seat.

In 1988, Lee & Associates started making preparations to open our first office in Los Angeles. I didn't know the area, so one day I set out and started driving L.A. I wanted to get to know the territory that we would soon be working.

While I was out, I noticed three warehouses. They were distinct because they were extremely tall, towering over everything else in the area.

Intrigued, I stopped at each building, knocked on the door, and asked about the how and why they were so much taller than other warehouses in the area. The owners of the buildings told me about this new business concept called "just-in-time" delivery, and these were the warehouses that supported it. Retailers wanted to minimize the size of their retail store footprints while creating bigger showrooms. They didn't want expensive retail space for their on-site warehouse; it didn't make sense. So they built these bigger, taller warehouses to store most of the product within close distance to the retail location. The objective was to deliver product from the manufacturer to the retailer just in time, right when it was needed, with little to no surplus on hand.

Around this time, there was also a change in sprinkler technology for fire prevention. Before this technology change, products could only be stored at a certain height for fire safety reasons. In the event of a fire, product stacked too high in a warehouse would limit the effectiveness of the sprinklers. With new technology, which monitored water flow, came the ability to store products higher, leading to these taller warehouses.

Suddenly, a light went on for me. I quickly realized that Los Angeles was about to need some build-to-suit warehouses because what existed in the market wasn't even close to where the future was headed. Warehouses were small and had low-ceiling clearance by comparison. This just-in-time delivery model would take off quickly, and I knew I had spotted this trend early. I had gotten ahead of a huge shift in the market. I was going to use it to my advantage to position the new Lee & Associates office at the cutting edge.

I had a vision for warehouses in Los Angeles and the way they would impact the market. But it wasn't enough just to have that vision. I had to support it and get on top of it so that I could put myself in the best possible position.

So for the next six months, I worked to put together a presentation about the coming trend in warehouse build-to-suits. I spent hours researching; I brought in a bunch of experts, wrote reports, and compiled all my information. I was determined to be the expert on this trend, so I prepared and studied every aspect of it.

At the end of those six months, I had tremendous confidence in my vision because I had done the necessary preparation. I was ready to act upon it and share it with others.

Taking the time to wander in your market and go to places you may not usually go can help you see the world differently. And seeing the world differently is the forerunner of vision. Without vision, it's impossible to get ahead of upcoming trends and use them to your advantage.

Recognize that your vision won't always be right, it won't always be exactly what happens (see the chapter "Best Laid Plans" for how my bright idea about warehouses stalled before it unstalled). But you want to support it, internalize it, believe in it, and be able to communicate it to others. When you believe in your vision in this way, you increase your self-confidence because every action you take aligns with this belief. If you commit to your vision fully, the things you need to do become that much clearer.

Thinking about what's going to happen and coming up with an idea of where you see the future going also allows you to merge your personal vision with your professional one. When your professional vision informs your personal vision, you will be better equipped to make all your dreams come true. So continually take the time to map out where you believe the industry is headed, and how you can get out ahead to help you move forward on the path to excellence.

CHAPTER 40

TODAY YOU MIGHT SUCK

Bill Lee

In the twenty-five years that I coached youth basketball, I probably had more than fifty teams (understand, I had three sons who all played hoops throughout high school). Most of my teams, however, were made up of seventh and eighth graders. Most of these kids attended Catholic schools that were situated in an extremely competitive basketball program in Orange County, California. Private and public high schools in the area recruited from this league, so it was an important time for these kids to hone and demonstrate their skills. It was also a wonderful age to coach young men.

The boys I coached typically came from upper-middle-class backgrounds. They went to good schools, practiced in nice gyms, and had the time and resources to pursue the game.

Now, with a minimum of ten players on each team, I had the difficult job of making sure each kid got enough playing time. I wanted to give them all the chance to play in real games, and also appease the parents in the stands, which was one of the harder parts of the coaching job. I would have the kids play in three tournaments, a pre-season, and a league season, and we would also always go to the playoffs. Our seasons, then, would have at least thirty games, plus, when the season ended, I would enter my 7th graders in the recreation department's Spring League. It was not unusual for me to coach as many as sixty to eighty games in a season, especially when all three of my sons were playing at the same time. And I loved it!

One year, I had a great kid on my team named Matt McGraw. He came from a tight-knit, Catholic family, and was one of five boys. You couldn't help but like Matt. He had a great personality. He was bright and outgoing, energetic and precocious. I knew his family, having coached his brothers before, and he stands out today in my mind as one of my favorite players.

Matt was a good kid but an average basketball player. He knew the fundamentals and he could hold his own on the court, but he wasn't a star. Which is fine because I'd seen many average players go on to become star players in high school and college, and vice versa—tons of young stars losing their edge later on. At this age level, it's hard to tell who has what it takes to make it. But Matt was certainly a very determined, hard-working kid.

During one game, I was making a lot of substitutions to ensure everyone got his time on the court. I sent Matt into the game before realizing another kid on the team hadn't had his chance to play yet. After about two minutes, I pulled Matt and subbed in the other kid.

Matt made his way down the bench to sit next to me, his sweaty brows furrowed. Absorbed in the game, I just gave him a vague smile. But after a minute or so, he couldn't hold it in anymore. He burst out, "Coach Lee, I suck today!"

I looked at him, surprised and trying very hard not to laugh. It's extremely unusual for a kid to say something like that. I got a lot of kids who vehemently believed in just the opposite; a lot of kids who knew they were the next Kobe Bryant or Michael Jordan. Heck, I got a lot of parents boasting about how amazing and special their boys were. Very rarely did I have a kid openly admit that he sucked.

I've found that the same is true of salespeople. How many business people do you know who can say, "I suck today"? The truth is that many can't! They have this all-consuming ego that doesn't allow them to admit they are failing. What they don't realize is that ego is what's holding them back in the end.

To achieve a life of excellence, you have to accept that today you might suck. Today, you may fail. Today, you may lose. You have to be willing to admit that you aren't perfect, and recognize your mistakes when you make them and then get better.

When your ego gets in the way and blinds you to the things you do wrong, you can't move forward. When you pretend you didn't fail or try to cover up your loss with fake positivity, you're only ignoring the problem. It's like ignoring the symptoms of an oncoming cold. The cold is only going to get worse unless you take the time to make yourself better. In the same way, you will never achieve excellence if you can't admit your failures and fix them.

Admitting "I suck today" might strike many as pessimistic, self-defeating, or just mean. But when I say you have to accept that "today I suck," it does not mean tearing yourself down. There's a difference between admitting your failure and beating yourself up about it. Saying, "I suck today" allows you to take an honest look at what you're doing wrong. Only by admitting that we failed can we then do something about it.

The people who can't take this first step, who can't acknowledge their failure, are the ones who never move past it. But if you can accept your failure without letting it get you down, you will be much closer to your path to excellence. Those who accept that they've failed find more possibilities for excellence than those who stubbornly insist that everything is fine.

It happens to all of us. Years ago, I was brought into a presentation by one of our salespeople. It was for a big deal that involved prime industrial property in the center of Southern California, a market where there was an extremely limited supply of land. Whoever got the listing would be able to see every major build-to-suit in the marketplace. This is a huge advantage because then you know what buildings will become vacant and have an opportunity for large fees.

Additionally, the site was large enough that if you enhanced your relationship with the ownership, you would have a base of business for years and years to come marketing the land and the future buildings.

My fatal flaw was that I analyzed the ownership as uninformed and, in doing so, put a presentation together to inform them that we knew how to capitalize on the opportunities that arose. In hindsight, the ownership was very intelligent, and had done their homework on the asset they owned. They were looking for a broker who was going to bring them the business, not tell them the process. I talked too much and didn't deliver on the essence of what the client wanted to hear.

So now, in a moment of truth, I'll admit it… I sucked at the presentation. I talked too much and tried to teach the client rather than sell the client. It still haunts me to this day but I was too big at the time to admit that I sucked. There, I feel better already!

CHAPTER 41

BEST LAID PLANS

Bill Lee

I've said it before, and I'll say it again; preparation is the name of the game. When you're working on a project, or acting on your vision for the future, you have to put in the time and attention to make sure you are covered for everything.

But as you might already know, even the best-laid plans can be tipped on their heads when life throws a curveball. Sometimes you do everything right, and for whatever reason the world just says, "No."

When this happens, it's easy to get discouraged. Don't worry, your day will come. But part of having a vision is making sure you prepare for these worst-case scenarios. They aren't fun to think about, but anticipating these roadblocks and creating strategies to counteract them will help soften the blow when they do hit.

In 1989, I finished up my project on build-to-suit warehouses and just-in-time delivery. I had spent six months researching, interviewing experts, planning, and preparing for every possible scenario—except for what happened next.

If you know your history, you know that in September of 1989, our country went into a significant recession. Companies began downsizing, warehouses emptying out, and my carefully thought-out plans for huge warehouses went down the recessionary drain.

No one was thinking about building much of anything, let alone build-to-suits. Investing in large warehouses was the last thing on investors' minds when every financial advisor and broker was telling them to limit their liabilities and save, rather than spend. During this recession, vacancy for warehouses jumped to nearly 25 percent in Southern California. No one was in the market for big warehouses.

I was a lone voice telling people to do something different. I had done all the homework and had the research to support my idea, but it was a recession; suddenly, the research didn't matter anymore. No one wanted to listen to me talk about warehouses and just-in-time delivery when they were dealing with falling stock prices, consumers who weren't spending, vacancy, and layoffs.

The project died. My six months of work disappeared, and I can't tell you how disappointing and frustrating it was. I had been so sure that I was right, that I was on to the next big trend in industrial development—in this case, warehouses. Even though the stagnant market was a reality and warehouse space wasn't leasing, shifting my focus was difficult. I had trouble letting go of my idea, especially after spending so much time on it. I was confident that the market would turn eventually, and I truly believed we would be ahead of the game.

So I started making pitches to be the leasing agent to the many owners of vacant industrial space. Whether they were owners or users looking to sublease didn't matter, because I felt if I had enough space under control that I would feel the turnaround in the market before my competitors.

As part of my just-in-time delivery project, I studied the number of pallets you could get in buildings of varying size with varying sizes of pallet positions. I created a graph showing these numbers. When I went to pitch a listing, I would tell the owner how his building compared to others of similar size. Now, rarely did a user ask how many pallet positions he could get in a building. Heck, many of the deal makers didn't even know their own average pallet position size—but wow, did the institutional owners love the idea! It was just another trivia fact that these MBAs could run to their bosses to gain favor.

Mr. Lee had just become their new favorite broker, and overnight I had 3,000,000 square feet of listings—listings that allowed me to feel the pulse of the distribution market as it battled through a recession and then positioned itself for build-to-suits for the coming of the new high-tech warehouses.

So the moral of the story is, don't give up hope when the worst case hits. Fight to hold your ground and live for another day.

Having the knowledge and the vision for the future of warehouse space allowed me to see who came back to the market first. It allowed me to be sitting on top when the nation came out of the recession. I had the space, became the go-to expert with the space, and had the research to back up my claims.

So do the work. Prepare for every scenario. The hard work will pay off eventually, even if it's not in the way you want or at the precise moment you want. You might still learn a valuable lesson from your failed vision, one that will better equip you to handle future curveballs that are sure to come.

CHAPTER 42

SOMETIMES THINGS JUST DON'T GO YOUR WAY

Bill Lee

Let's talk some more about mistakes, because we all make them. Some are funny in the moment, some are funny after the fact, and some are just truly devastating. But the point is, they're going to happen. Somewhere along this journey, you are going to make a left-hand turn when you should have made a right. It happens, and in knowing that, the point is not to do everything in your power to avoid these mistakes. The point is to be prepared for mistakes, and open to learning new lessons from them when they happen. That's how we grow.

In our business, many people work under the false belief that the truly excellent brokers achieved success because they didn't make any mistakes. How many times have you looked at someone who, in your eyes, is beyond successful, and thought that he or she could do no wrong?

Well, I guarantee you that anyone with any semblance of success in this world got there only by making mistakes, and plenty of them. In fact, like the old saying, "The higher you rise, the harder you fall," the more successful you are, the bigger your mistakes become.

Shortly after we started Lee & Associates, one of the guys whose father lived in Southern California came to me with a sure-fire idea.

"Bill," he said to me, "my dad has a friend in the Mexican government who has given him a great scoop. There's been a flight of capital out of Mexico, because a lot of people are worried about the economy. These individuals have been buying real estate in California, Texas, and Florida, but the Mexican government wants that money back in the country.

"What they want is to put the real estate into a trust overseen by the Mexican government until the property can be resold. The motivation to sell is that the Mexican government is going to double tax the property if they don't. The government wants one company to go out and broker these equities that were purchased in the U.S. The individuals are to hire this company to transact the business, and the money will go back into the trust governed by the individuals and the government to get the money back in Mexico."

My interest was immediately piqued.

"What kind of money are we talking here?" I asked.

"Six billion dollars' worth of properties," said he.

I was blown away. That was big money, especially to our little, brand-new company. I got a fire in my stomach, the familiar competitive edge kicking in. I wanted this deal!

He went on to tell me that this group of men from the Mexican government wanted to meet us. So we immediately dropped everything and scraped together all our excess cash, which was not much back then, and brought the men out for a visit. We put them up in a hotel in Orange County, and wined and dined them for three days. I even broke out Spanish 1A from my high school days.

Our effort was well-received, and they liked us well enough to invite me to come down to Mexico a few weeks later. In the meantime, I took a crash course in Spanish 1B, trying to learn the language so that I could communicate once I got there (ha!). Nothing else mattered during this frantic and heady time. The number they had given me—that "6" followed by a "B"—blinded me to all else. I had never been more excited, nor had my partners.

I flew from Los Angeles to Mexico City and met with all these folks. At the end of the visit, they gave me an inch-thick contract in Spanish. I was thrilled. Even though I couldn't read it, I came back to the States thinking we had landed the deal. I gave the contract to my attorney, who gave it to his interpreter. It took us a few weeks, but eventually we sent it back. By the time we sent it back, we'd been communicating with them for four months, start to finish. But $6 billion is well worth four months and some pretty hefty attorney fees for a young company like ours at the time. It was a whirlwind. My partners and I had many conversations about what we could do with our coming commission dollars. Oh my, what fun we had talking about this deal.

And then—we never heard from them ever again. After we sent the contract we waited, and waited, and waited, but nothing ever happened. It turned out that the Mexican government did not have any legal grounds for imposing the added tax. So, we had spent four months of time, money, and resources on a group of government officials that had not vetted properly the concept of a double tax. We sat around expecting a $6 billion pay-off, and all we got was a good laugh (a laugh that has lasted thirty-five years, and counting).

This happens a lot in commercial real estate. We spend a lot of time on deals or wooing clients and little comes from it. Sometimes the effort does payoff, but the trick in real estate is learning how to value your time. What efforts are worth spending your time on and what efforts are not? It's not always easy to tell. We waste so much time working on things that, if we had been smart from the beginning, we might have realized were never going to pan out.

Learning to separate the viable deals from the people just wasting time is a whole other skill in itself on your path toward excellence. After all, time is precious. This sixth sense comes only with practice. And you will make mistakes, so just accept it—but if you are going to waste time, make sure that the time wasted is in your chosen specialty.

The way I see it, by the end of your career, if you don't have stories like the one I just told, you were playing it way too safe. You need to chase deals and just know that you're going to be wrong—but you might be right. When those wrong moments come, embrace them, learn what you can from them, and be prepared for more down the road. Mistakes are brutal. They're a kick in the face. But sometimes they're also the kick you need to get you going in the right direction—the direction that leads to excellence.

What is that right direction? Easy. Finding a particular focus on a segment of the market such that you can separate yourself from your competition by learning all there is to know about all aspects of that market segment. Only after you put yourself in that position and have the ability to manage the oversight of that market segment, should you venture into other market segment opportunities.

You are going to lose some or many of your opportunities by doing this. But if a deal is in your wheelhouse (your specific market segment) you have not wasted your time because you gained knowledge and relationships in that segment. But if you went out of your market segment and lost, your time was wasted because you won't be returning to it again anytime soon.

Our time spent on the Mexican transaction was all wasted. But then again, people spend a lot of money just to have a good laugh and that deal continues to make me laugh whenever I spend time with my original partners.

CHAPTER 43

FIND YOUR POWER SOURCE

Bill Lee

Spend any time in commercial real estate and you'll learn pretty fast that there are no sure things. Like the Mexico deal, you will encounter transactions that seem like they are going to fall your way, then take an awkward turn and collapse at the last minute. No one cares how much work you put into it or how much you were counting on that commission. When it's over, it can often feel like it's over for good.

The best brokers know how to handle failure. They know themselves enough to recognize a source of power that gets them through the low points. And they use it.

I've already told you about my incredible "mentor in disguise" John Sutherland. John taught me a lot in our time working together, and one of the greatest lessons I learned watching him was how to overcome failure.

John had two characteristics that really made him stand out as a broker: a devotion to cold calling, and an unrelenting personality. Basically, John wouldn't accept "no" for an answer.

John hated to lose a deal, especially if it was to a competing firm. If he lost a deal, it would ruin his whole day. I can only imagine what he was like when he got home at night. But instead of moping or getting angry, John had one powerful rule that he followed to help him recover from his losses.

The morning after losing a deal, John would come to the office at 4:30 a.m. and begin calling his East Coast contacts, hoping to catch someone at his or her desk before the switchboard opened up. He would continue his calls throughout the morning, working into the Midwest time zone, then the Mountain West time zone, and by 8:00 a.m., after already being on the phone for three and a half hours, he would begin with local contacts.

His goal was to replace the deal he lost with *three* prospective new deals by *lunch*. John knew his power was that he never took no for an answer and was perfectly comfortable dialing for dollars. He knew that instead of getting angry or upset about losing a deal, he had to channel that loss into a win. The only way he could get over failing was by winning.

So what's your power source? What motivates you to spring back after a failure? Yes, today you might suck, but you shouldn't stop there. Find what drives you to turn your loss into a win, make it a habit, and continue to drive down the path to excellence.

Maybe, like John, you push yourself harder to achieve a new deal. Maybe your power source is going home to your family after a rough day of losing, and allowing their love and support to motivate you to keep going. Maybe it's going to dinner with a mentor to discuss the loss, and picking his or her brain on how to move forward.

Whatever it is, find your power source. Don't let the fear of failing again keep you from pursuing the path of excellence.

And yes, I followed John Sutherland's 4:30 a.m. strategy, and not only did it work, but it led to many more deals than just three, time and time again.

CHAPTER 44
A CAREER OF BASE HITS
R. Craig Coppola

If we're talking about mistakes, I have more than my fair share. But I've always found that it's the way you react to those mistakes, and the lessons you learn from them, that can and should have a bigger impact on your career.

In the early years of my career, I had one thought that I am sure you have had at some point in your life: I need to make money.

At the time, I was just beginning my career as a commercial real estate broker and I was doing small monetary transactions to stay afloat. They were the small, one-off deals of a few thousand square feet. Nothing that was going to make me rich, but necessary to pay the bills. Like many young brokers, I had my eye on the big deals. I called them my home run deals, and I was hungry for my first one.

Brokers have different ways of defining a big deal, depending on their markets or where they are in their careers. At the time I guess I dreamed big—my definition of a home run deal, and it hasn't changed much over the years, is a deal with a half-million to a million-dollar commission. I idolized the brokers who landed those deals. If I could only do what they were doing, maybe I would be on that side of success. So I mimicked their work habits, and dreamt of the day I would join the big leagues and start hitting my own home runs.

But just doing what they did wasn't enough. I wasn't successful for a long time. My shortcoming wasn't effort or drive. The problem was, I didn't have the experience or the relationships in the beginning. Still, I continued to work every year on a home run deal, knowing one day I would get there.

The first home run deal that I believed I had a legitimate shot at happened within my first four or five years in the business. It was 40,000-square-foot office space for Bell Atlantic, and after weeks of work, I thought for sure it was mine. I had built the relationship with the client. I knew the requirement inside and out. I had worked the pitch at the perfect angle. For the first time, I was sure that I'd landed it. It was a rush.

I remember making the pitch believing it was in the bag. "I nailed it," I thought as I walked out of the meeting. You can imagine how devastated I was when I lost the assignment. I went home that night and I was sick to my stomach. In fact, I was a wreck for the entire week after. In my mind I kept thinking, "This wasn't like the other home run deals I've worked on before, deals I knew I didn't have any real shot at. This wasn't a deal that I was just working on to learn. This was the first big deal I honestly thought I could land." I felt kicked down further than I had ever been kicked before.

What was worse, I really could have used the money from that deal. I had been banking on that commission. The shut-out was a serious blow.

At that moment, I swore to myself that I would never again need a transaction for survival. I would never rely on any one deal to pay my bills. I vowed to have so much business, so many relationships, that when I lost a deal, it wouldn't be devastating. It would be part of the game, a precursor to winning, rather than a shattering blow. The loss of the big deal I thought I had in the bag taught me a valuable lesson and changed by view of the business.

The next day when I walked in the office, I looked around at the guys who did three to four huge home run transactions a year. They were the ones I idolized and thought I would emulate. But because of my lesson, I realized I'd rather close one hundred base hits. I wanted to be in a position so that if I lost, whether a big deal or a little one, it wouldn't matter. That's not to say losing a deal wouldn't still hurt, because it did—I don't like to lose, ever. But I never again felt the despair and the desperation I felt at losing that first big deal.

I still kept that goal of landing a home run deal at the forefront of my mind, however. I wasn't discouraged from chasing more million-dollar commissions. I just made sure I had enough going on that if I didn't land those deals, I wouldn't suffer. It was a good plan that lasted.

For the next fifteen years, I made it a goal to always be working on a home run deal. Every year, I wanted to make sure I had a home run deal in the works. Whether we closed it or not didn't matter, but I had to have one at all times. It helped me keep my edge and kept me in the mix of the big action and the big leagues.

I have lost track of how many home run deals I worked on in the next years. They continued to die, but because I had my career of base hits supporting me, I could afford to let them go and look for the next one without wallowing. I was more concerned about where my next home run deal was coming from, knowing that one day, my work would pay off. One day, I was going to close one.

It took years, but eventually I closed my first home run deal. Then I closed another, and another. A goal I had carried with me for fifteen years finally paid off, and I found myself in the big leagues. I continued with my base hits, because those were my bread and butter, the foundation I'd built my career on. But now I had the experience and the confidence to land the big guys, and my career took off.

A career of base hits is just fine. In fact, you should always have your base hits to make sure you are secure enough to chase after the home runs. If you can hit those humdingers, by all means hit them. But don't depend on those deals. Don't depend on any one deal. The goal is to have enough business that you never have to worry about losing. Only that way can you win and achieve excellence in your career and any area of life you choose.

CHAPTER 45

CRITIQUE OR CRITICISM

Bill Lee

When you make a mistake, it's often a chance for a new direction or fresh start. But many times, it's also the chance for others to question and doubt you.

When I had the chance to hear Mike Vance, the Disney vendor-turned-"dean of creative thinking," speak all those years ago, he changed my life by teaching me how to harness my thoughts and put them into action. So many of his words and lessons have stuck with me to this day. One of his most important lessons is that there is no such thing as a bad idea. The only bad idea is the idea you never express because you're afraid of criticism.

"Every idea leads to another," he asserted. "Ideas are meant to be expressed, analyzed, categorized, or discarded."

I view criticism in the same way. For every critique you receive, analyze and implement it or discard it. Criticism is not the enemy, unless it freezes you up and prevents you from chasing your goals.

When someone makes a mistake, I manage my method for feedback. I tell the person that I value his or her intention, but that perhaps there's a way we could have done it even better. I provide a solution with the critique. Why? I never want to thwart initiative. Put yourself in the shoes of others in your office, maybe even your own shoes; some people are very sensitive and equate taking initiative with taking risk. That mindset has left too many adults slow or unable to take initiative because they fear failure.

The path to excellence demands your strength and confidence. If and when you achieve any level of success, you will find that jealousy will come from some, often in the form of criticism. They will tell you what you can't do and what you're doing the wrong way. Listen to them, but at the end of day believe in yourself. Make and own your decisions based on what you think is right. Live with the consequences of your initiative, both positive and negative, because that's the way to find excellence. Your failures can be equal or better teachers than your successes.

Personally, I don't like to be criticized. I can take critique, but I don't like even that. I learn best from asking others how they would handle various situations that I didn't do well in—that is, when I take the initiative to assess my performance rather than when someone else does. That's just me. I wish I were a bigger man, but it's my nature to value "doing" even if it is done the wrong way, and oftentimes I feel that being critiqued comes from someone who lacks the doing part.

On the other hand, I admit to being told, "Bill, maybe you should let a few days pass before you react to comments, critique, and criticism about your actions, because I think you might have a different interpretation of what has been said."

Taking a step back and absorbing comments allows you to make the distinction between criticism and critique, and identify who provides each. The dictionary says criticism is censure, disapproval, reproach, condemnation, and denunciation. People who criticize do not have good intentions, despite what they may believe. Often they want to see you fail, and speak only to wound.

Critique, however, is associated with words like evaluation, review, appraisal, and analysis. Don't they sound much more constructive and positive? People who offer critique tend to offer solutions or new ways of thinking. Their intent is to help you improve, rather than tear you down.

You have to learn to recognize people's intentions. Are they offering criticism or critique? Are they working to tear you down or help you out? You also have to distinguish between people who have some knowledge of and success in what they are talking about, and those who don't. Learning to discern these things helps you discover who to listen to and who to ignore. Criticism that is really critique is actually a good thing. Look forward to it and look forward to growing.

Today I own, in an LLC with others (including Craig), a bed and breakfast, and I serve as the manager of that LLC. We have 22 employees (landscapers, housekeepers, innkeepers and coffee shop employees) and it has become a time-consuming enterprise. For me it is a labor of love as the property is located right on the beautiful back bay of Morro Bay.

I'm not getting any younger and the work load is significant, which prompted me to ask a four-year employee, an innkeeper who was relocating, to write me a note suggesting what changes to the operation I should consider.

When she left she made sure to leave a note in my mailbox that said how much she enjoyed working at the B&B. And then, at the end, she said "This is a great place to work with the only problem being that there is no clear leadership or policies. If everyone knew who was in charge of what and consistent company polices, you would have less bickering between staff and the guests would have a more consistent experience."

I asked for the critique and she didn't hold back. Am I happy about it? You bet! I love the place and want it to be all that it can be.

How about you? Do you ask to be critiqued regularly? Is your ego so fragile that you don't like hearing that you might not be perfect? The point is to understand the difference between criticism and critique and embrace critique, because it can only make you better.

Steve Silk (Eastdil Secured)

Steve is another street broker, innovator, and self-actualizing broker who has attained immense success. Steve has never stopped thinking and creating, though he has reached the pinnacle of success in the world of institutional investment sales.

His path to excellence started with a local firm in the Los Angeles International Airport area of Southern California. While schlepping door-to-door in the world of industrial real estate, he was mentored by the early "who's who" of knowledgeable commercial realtors in that area.

He continued his industrial real estate brokerage excellence at Cushman & Wakefield and as a thinker, recognized a significant shift in institutional investment sales when institutions began buying from institutions but needed support information to authenticate their purchases.

Steve moved to Secured Capital with his partner Jay Borzi, and together they built a tremendous support team to capitalize on this trend, attaining great success such that Eastdil made them an offer to purchase that they couldn't refuse. They built a platform focused on institutional sales and purchases. Steve is still going strong brokering major transactions across the United States and having fun while mentoring young adults at the USC School of Business.

Eastdil Secured, now a member of the Wells Fargo Bank family, offers a tremendous platform in the investment discipline, debt placement, investment banking, mortgage loan sales, private equity JV transactions, and corporate real estate transactions as a member of the largest real estate investment bank in the world.

SECTION IV:
SHARE EXCELLENCE

PLATFORM PROFILE
Roger Staubach (Jones Lang LaSalle, Inc.)

Roger is a leader in every walk of life—family, sports, military, and business. There is a saying, "I would rather have them talk about me than say it myself," and Roger is that man. A true gentleman, he is revered by his colleagues and loved by his family and friends. Just ask any JLL employee that worked for the Staubach Company and they will tell you how they revere him. One quality that stood out for me when I met with him was his humility. For a man who has accomplished so much, and in a world (CRE) where humility is in short supply, it was very refreshing. Then again, I thought, humility goes hand in hand with leadership and that encapsulates who he is.....a leader!

As a leader, innovator, and deal maker in commercial real estate, he accurately recognized the value of starting a firm soley focused on tenant representation. While playing professional football for the Dallas Cowboys, he recognized that need for focused service organization in the market and started the Staubach Company in Dallas, Texas. Through a client-first mentality, he achieved great national success at the Staubach Company such that he led all other firms in the industry in attempting to replicate this strategy as specific focus and over forty years later, these firms are still playing catch up.

Happy at Jones, Lang, LaSalle, he also, is still going strong at age seventy-three. He just passed his earn out, continues to provide leadership to the firm, is still married to his 5th grade girlfriend fifty years later, and still quarterbacking his family flag football team which consists of four children and seven grandchildren.

Roger capitalized on a platform of celebrity, and built a company around a fundamental understanding of service to the client that he acquired in his early days as a street broker. He was able to harness his focus into a national organization with a cooperative spirit that emanated from his innate leadership strengths; strengths that we all saw lead him to the Heisman Trophy at Navy and three Super Bowl rings as the quarterback of the Dallas Cowboys.

JLL, a public company, provides a national platform of excellence today across the United States and worldwide in 200 corporate offices worldwide offering services in: consulting, lease administration, tenant representation, transaction management, development services & facilities management.

CHAPTER 46

THE FOUR LEVELS
OF REFERRALS

R. Craig Coppola

How do you measure excellence? You've put in the long hours of work, landed a few notable transactions, built a successful resume, achieved some goals, and are feeling pretty good about yourself. In your eyes, you're worthy of the title of "excellence." But what do other people think?

As Bill and I have said time and time again, the business of brokerage depends on relationships, others' and your own. Utilizing your business and social connections is one of the best ways to bring in new business and expand your reach. It is also one of the best ways to discover if you are achieving true excellence. The truth of the matter is, you can think anything you want about yourself, but it's what others think about you, your performance, your professionalism, and more that matters most to your success.

An excellent measure of success, it turns out, is actually as simple as the quality of referrals you receive from your clients and the people around you. The holy grail of our business and countless others is to garner as many strong referrals as possible. It makes our lives so much easier. But all referrals are not created equal. To truly measure the level of excellence you've achieved, take a look at the level of referrals you get from other people. Referrals go much further than simply passing along contact information. Over the years, I've discovered four different levels of referrals that guide me in my quest toward excellence. And it matters which ones I receive.

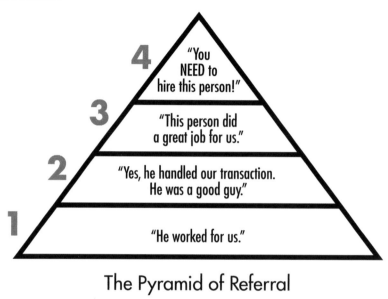

The Pyramid of Referral

First Level: "He worked for us."

> This type of referral is the most basic. One person you've worked with tells an associate that you worked together. That's it. Just a simple answer with no elaboration on what kind of worker you are or how well you performed. Oftentimes, this is a polite way to say you had no lasting impact on them, negative or positive. Think of it as politically correct.

Second Level: "Yes, he handled our transaction. He was a good guy."

> This referral is a step above the first level, but not by much. You get a positive statement that you were likable, but there's no strong emotion behind it. And there's no indication of how effective you

were on the job. The referrer simply liked you, which is nice, but not enough to guarantee that a contact will want to work with you. Like is not the same thing as trust.

Third Level: "This person did a great job for us."

The third level dives into the actual work you did, and receives a positive review. It's a nice review of your skills, and you might feel pretty good after receiving such a referral. Someone might be willing to hire you at this level, but it's not the highest level you could achieve.

Fourth Level: "You NEED to hire this person!"

Your phone usually rings after this type of referral. Enough said on that.

You see the difference between "This person did a good job" and "You'd be a fool not to hire this person"? The fourth level referral is passionate and strong. The person referring you truly believes that everyone needs to work with you, and at the very least, to meet you. When you start getting fourth level referrals, that's when you know your excellence is being noticed by others.

How do you get this type of referral? You provide service that is so good, your client can't give you anything else. If you want that level of referral, you have to do that level of work. You make yourself unforgettable. It's all about adding exceptional value, going above and beyond for a client so that shouting your merits from the rooftops becomes spontaneous. People simply can't help themselves.

Our business survives off referrals. You can make a living on level two and three referrals, but if you're on the journey to excellence, you can make a career on level four referrals.

CHAPTER 47

EXCELLENCE CULTURE PYRAMID

Bill Lee

As the contents of this book have affirmed time and time again, excellence is a journey. And like any true journey, you need a roadmap.

Below, I have included a diagram of my Excellence Culture Pyramid, with the building blocks for creating a culture of excellence. The main inspiration for this pyramid comes from John Wooden, whose original Pyramid of Success you can find here: http://www.coachwooden.com/pyramid-of-success

Many of these items we have discussed directly or indirectly in this book, and are summarized and presented in this neat graph. As with the pyramids of the great Egyptians, every block must be balanced or the whole thing will come tumbling down. Every aspect of excellence that we've discussed requires your attention and care, otherwise the whole thing cannot stand.

You can use this pyramid as a checklist to make sure you are creating a balanced culture of excellence. Or you can create one of your own, drawing on the lessons in this book and your personal priorities to map out excellence in your life.

The Excellence Culture Pyramid recognizes two cornerstones in its foundation: spirituality and thought.

1. **Spirituality:** It would be easy for me to say that you are either a believer or non-believer, but then I might seem very limited in my perspective. There are so many perspectives on spirituality that it would not be right for me to do this, so I will acknowledge the existence and value of a spiritual non-believer. It doesn't matter which you are. The bottom line of spirituality in the concept of seeking excellence is knowing that this journey is a set path. You assume that you are following the direction of whatever spiritual concept you believe in. This provides you with the courage and confidence to proceed to take action, knowing that you are being guided in your actions by something greater than yourself.

   Furthermore, whatever the result, you can accept it and give thanks with the knowledge that it was meant to be, whether a successful outcome or an outcome without the desired result. For me, it all begins, and ends with the belief in the existence of God and the teachings of Jesus Christ. But for you, it might be another religious authority, or a belief in the greater cosmic working of the universe. Whatever your spirituality, don't separate it from this journey to excellence. Rather, integrate it into your routine and let it guide you to success.

2. **Thought:** Oh my, the wasted time and energy that takes place in this world without the benefit of prior thought. When you strive to include excellence in several different areas, such as career, family, and sports, within the umbrella of excellence in life, the overwhelming obstacle of time rears its head. How is it possible to spread this excellence to all relevant aspects of our life when we have only so many hours in the day? Every day must start

with thought and careful planning until our habits become so refined that proper decision-making becomes rote, solidified through years of practice.

Foundations have to last the test of time and provide the basis for the culture to mature, so this foundation continues with Support and Health.

3. **Support:** We are all good at performing some things, and not so good at others. We can be experienced in some matters and lost in others. Certainly, one of your most important support people can be your spouse, but how deep is the rest of your "bench"? As good as John Wooden was, he needed three great assistant coaches to run the streak: Crum, Norman, and Cunningham. And as good as Bill Russell was, Red Auerbach was his equal in his domain, and what a great cast of teammates they both had at their disposal. Support in life comes from all directions: a personal assistant, a minister, teachers, banker, accountant, lawyer, entrepreneur, peer, Google, books, YouTube, counselor, advisor coach, etc. Build that network to support your excellence culture, and make that support group your unpaid board of directors, always finding ways to help each of them in return for what you ask of them.

4. **Health (Mental and Physical):** Step one toward a disciplined life is good health. In this journey, make time to properly care for yourself, mentally and physically. Often, health is one of the first sacrifices you make in order to chase excellence, but watch how quickly the rest of your pyramid falls when you lack proper rest or nutrition. Give yourself enough time to rest, create balance in your life, and make sure you nurture your body so that you can perform at your very best.

A culture matures from its foundation, and from it flows Integration, Attitude, and Discipline.

5. **Integration:** It is necessary to balance the priorities of family, health, organization, equity, responsibility, spirituality, and duty.

6. **Attitude:** Attitude defines interactive behavior and sets the tone for respect, integrity, humility, efficiency, and thoroughness. Without the right attitude, you will go through the motions but never make a true impact on yourself or others.

7. **Discipline:** Allowing you to execute the necessities of each endeavor, discipline transfers to all aspects of life. It is contagious. Discipline in diet transfers to discipline in exercise, which transfers to work habits, which transfers to the family, which transfers to fun and relaxation, which transfers to attitude, and attitude begins the cycle all over again.

And soon results start to happen, building the rest of the pyramid with Direction and Preparedness.

8. **Direction:** A defined highway directs the route to success. Know where you want to go, and you will find it is much easier to get there. You cannot hope to find your end destination with a broken compass. Make sure you know where true north is, and follow your journey to your end goal.

9. **Preparedness:** Preparedness is the vehicle that delivers the goods. Without preparation, all your good intentions mean nothing. Having a goal is one thing, but acting on that goal and laying out the steps to reach it is quite another. Preparation, coupled with thought, will allow you to build the blocks to your future success.

And finally comes recognition that a culture of excellence has been created.

10. **Acknowledgement:** The top of the pyramid is recognition from those involved in the enterprise—be it family, peers, associates, team members, a community at large, or just you—that you paid the price to create a culture of excellence.

Take the time to define and visualize what each building block in the pyramid means to you. Then, as you move along this path to excellence, make sure you maintain balance, giving proper attention and care to each part of the pyramid to ensure it stays strong and grows tall.

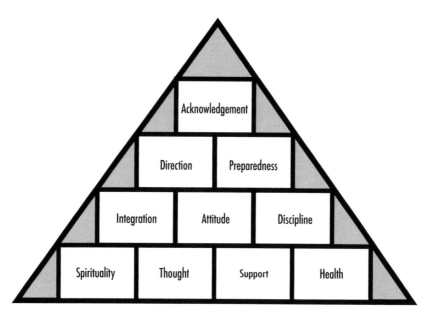

Excellence Culture Pyramid

CHAPTER 48

THE RAT PACK

R. Craig Coppola

For many years, Bill and I have both carried the title of "coach." Bill coached basketball teams for his three sons and for 7th and 8th grade boys. I followed in the footsteps of my father and became a baseball coach for my son and a group of his friends, first in Little League and then through a year-round club team we named The Arcadia Rat Pack.

The Rat Pack was born when a few neighborhood dads came together and lamented the absence of opportunities for our kids to play quality baseball in our area. We decided to form a year-round travel baseball team (a team that traveled to play the best teams in the country) of neighborhood kids—our sons and their friends. We brought together twelve local boys and coached them from age eight to fifteen, when they entered high school.

For seven years we played year-round, in more than thirty national tournaments as well as in local tournament games. When we started, we were in the lowest division and lost all our games in our first tournament. Four years later, we had improved enough to win our Little League district tournament (the first time our neighborhood had won in twenty years) and went on to finish second in the state tournament. By our final year, we were traveling all over the country, playing everyone and winning most of our games. Out of the thirty tournaments we entered, we placed in the top three in sixteen of them.

But what made this team truly special was not the number of wins, or even the marked improvement of these boys athletically over time. Rather, it was the lessons and values that we instilled in our players, and our hopes of starting them on their own paths to excellence.

The purpose of this team was not to breed superstar baseball players. These were just kids from our neighborhood—our sons' friends and family friends. We didn't cherry-pick the best players, because the initial focus of the team was not about winning all the time. Instead, our goal was to pass on lessons of excellence and demonstrate the value of commitment and hard work. We wanted to create a family that included not only these twelve boys and the coaches, but their entire families and the greater Arcadia neighborhood. We wanted to be leaders in the community, so we decided to do things a little differently from most baseball teams in this age group.

For example, we brought in several outside coaches to help us teach different aspects of the game. Now, I had played professionally and I was good, but I knew I was a better planner and committer than I was a coach. I knew my weaknesses. I played first base, but I knew nothing about pitching. So we brought in outside experts to address specific areas. We brought in former Major League pitcher, Mark Littell, to teach pitching; former Minor League hitting coach, Tony Dello to teach hitting; and Grand Canyon University Track Coach, Tom Flood, as a speed coach. A few of our kids learned how to be switch hitters. I brought up my dad, the ultimate baseball coach, and Jim Wing, former University of Arizona baseball coach, who used their vast years of experience to help us come together as a cohesive team.

We didn't profess to be experts. Rather, we taught our boys that if you don't know how to do something, bring in someone who does. Learn to surround yourself with coaches, mentors, and teachers who will help guide you to improve in various parts of your life.

Another thing we did was arrange college visits. What was unique was, we did these while the kids were still in middle school. We knew we would end the Rat Pack when the boys reached high school and joined their respective high school teams. But I wanted to address the idea of college and show these boys the value of setting long-term goals, the kind of long-term goals I set for myself when I was in high school. College was a tangible example of thinking ahead and planning for a brighter future.

Over the next few years, as a team we visited fifteen universities across the country. At every school, we toured the baseball facilities and met the coaches, but also looked at the campuses. We showed these boys that each and every one of them belonged at those schools and could compete athletically on that level if they worked hard enough. We instilled a futuristic mindset in them early on, and allowed them to visualize the possibilities.

Nine of those twelve kids played college sports. But not all of them are baseball players. One was a swimmer, one plays tennis for a Top Ten school, and one is a basketball player who was named Player of the Year in his conference as a sophomore. Again, this team had not been about breeding all-star baseball players. Baseball was just the sport we used to teach the boys bigger lessons, such as the value of commitment, goal setting, and determination. We wanted to give them the skills to have success, in any endeavor they chose.

We talk about sharing and giving excellence, and the Rat Pack is the example of sharing excellence that I'm most proud of. We taught these kids the value of excellence. We created a family, a bond that lasts to this day.

We recently had a reunion, and putting them together and seeing how well they are doing was humbling and rewarding. They have grown into outstanding young men, and I'm incredibly proud of these kids. I have greatly enjoyed watching them grow and embrace excellence in their own lives.

Sharing excellence with the next generation, creating a culture of excellence for them and teaching them these lessons, is one of the most rewarding things in life. Whether it's with your own kids, kids in your neighborhood, a sports team, a youth program like Big Brothers Big Sisters, or some other avenue, there are plenty of opportunities to pass excellence on.

And for those of you who doubt the value of mentoring the next generation, just remember who was there for you when you were that age. Our future is in the hands of these young people. They will be the ones running our country one day, and what better way to leave a legacy that ensures a brighter future than by sharing the lessons of excellence with the next generation?

CHAPTER 49

THE LEE & ASSOCIATES PLATFORM

Bill Lee

In 2007 and 2008, the most valuable player in the National Basketball Association was Steve Nash. Steve stood at barely six foot two, rarely jumped high enough to "stuff" the basketball, and was not particularly fast or strong. Yet he was selected by his peers to be the most valuable player in the league, an honor even more remarkable because his team did not win the championship in either year.

Those who knew Steve would say that he was driven to maximize his basketball skills and that, each year during the off season, he would add a new dimension to his game that would make him even better than the year before. He retired in 2014 after he entered the league as a second-round draft pick What made him an all-star and the most valuable player of the league was his unique ability to make those around him better players by his unselfish desire to create opportunities for them to score off his court leadership. He led the league in assists a remarkable ten years.

Steve attained his own excellence by supporting and making possible the excellence of others. He embraced the idea of sharing success, of creating a culture of winning, and giving it to others.

Now that you've committed to commit, changed your focus to compete against yourself and not others, and surrounded yourself with a support network of peers and friends, then becoming a leader who creates and shares a culture of excellence should be your natural next step.

Being a leader has nothing to do with your job title. You don't have to be the CEO of your company, or even a manager. In fact, a leader shares many similarities with a mentor (which we've discussed in previous chapters) but is more visible, and inspires and guides more than one person. You can be a leader in the office, stepping up to motivate others to achieve a company goal; a leader in the community, donating your time and services to helping local charities grow and thrive; a leader at home, setting a positive example for your children and family.

A leader takes this idea one step further, however, and not only inspires others by his, or her own, excellence, but deliberately creates a culture of excellence that others can share in. Being a leader means being selfless with your achievements, and creating a platform for excellence within your team, your office, your market, or your family.

One of the early marketing ads for Lee & Associates had the tagline, "Bill Lee founded a company, and then gave it away."

Essentially that's exactly what we did. When starting Lee & Associates, we had a vision of what it could become: an independent brokerage company providing services through a shared equal ownership, such that it included input from all those in the workplace. We believed that this structure would enable us to provide the client with a complete look at the market opportunities, an information resource, and a cooperative spirit that benefited all transactional people in their daily pursuit of successful brokerage.

I put up all the capital for the first office, but all of the founding partners were equal owners without putting up any money. We all had the same vote, and the only difference in status was that I had my name on the door. We viewed this partnership, and eventual corporation, as a conduit for the success of the individual broker. A broker that every year could extract his, or her, individual profitability out of the net profit from the office they worked in.

This partnership was comprised of individuals, many of whom were personal friends, and within the first four months we amassed ten partners, ten equal partners. We each had one vote and we acted only on a minimum 75 percent majority vote. We split profits to the individuals in the same percentage as each member's commissions equated to gross revenue. We raised capital to start future offices from the partners of the new, and existing locations, and paid them back annually, over the entire life of the entity, as a percentage of the gross revenue generated each year by each office.

Every salesperson we hired was given revenue goals, and when met, they automatically vested into the ownership of the office as a partner (later as a shareholder). We allowed every shareholder in every office to invest in the venture capital pool for every new office. In this way, we encouraged every owner to be interested in the success of every office. We encouraged our brokers to invest their annual bonus in real estate, an investment alternative that they knew and have specific knowledge of. We still encourage both of these things today.

It was, and still is, in my opinion, a win-win for the owners of each office, the salespeople hired into each office and the clients we serve that benefit from the shared service environment, and the investors providing the start-up capital for each office. Essentially, it is a win-win for everyone because everyone has a vested interest in the ongoing success of the individual office and the organization at large. Every salesperson had, has, or will have, a voice in the direction of the office they work out of takes. So support, location, information, services, new hires, management, expense control, etc., all come as a byproduct of the structure, allowing for every decision to be a group decision.

This platform is radically different than many other equally successful companies, But for Lee & Associates, it works. All fifty-plus locations across the country, all 900-plus salespeople, 450-plus shareholders sharing profits and investing in future locations, thirty-six years of history, and the structure still makes sense for us. It's a platform of excellence that builds on itself, creating a culture of success for a large majority of the brokers who join us.

My friend and fellow shareholder, R. Craig Coppola, has shared with me, while writing this book, that he has made more than enough in added commissions that he could have retired ten years earlier than if he had stayed at his previous company. Think about that! A decade! Think about how a cooperative spirit develops when you own a business equally with others and are genuinely interested in their success. Think how you would share information, share resources, purchase assets, and be of counsel to those around you.

This is an example of the kind of culture of excellence you should be able to create. I don't go into the specifics and successes of Lee & Associates to prop myself and our company up. Rather, it serves as an example of what can happen when one person, supported by a group of incredible partners, friends, and family members, decides to chase excellence with "out of the box" thinking and then build a platform of excellence that passes those lessons and achievements on to others. You too can do the same. Your platform can and will look very different from ours, but can and will be just as if not more successful. Whether it's through a company structure, a team structure, or relationships with those in your network, you can create a culture of excellence that can be shared to build something amazing.

I have a tremendous fondness for my peers, those obviously with Lee & Associates but also those who work for our competitors as well. We all have one thing in common; we get paid only on performance. We start every year on the same starting line marked zero and we go out and make it happen. How can you not respect the people you work with, and against, that exist in this kind of transaction world?

I respect the firms that these salespeople work for and the platforms that they provide for their salespeople. These platforms vary and offer different benefits to the various salespeople that work in this marketplace, but all in all it is a very sharing marketplace and the platforms of every firm offers value to its employees, albeit differing value. And all of these platforms began with one person chasing excellence and wanting to share that excellence with others. Imagine that!

I've retired now. I miss the battles and competition, the camaraderie, the highs, and even the lows. And I'm proud of the Lee organization, not because it bears my name, not because we built it, but because of what it stands for. It was built by working salespeople, with their own money, and they were bold enough to try something new. They went out of the box to chase excellence, starting on the streets of Southern California, and spreading out across the country.

I remember the early days when we opened the first office in September, 1979 in Irvine, California. We had as good a nucleus as was ever possible to put together: Al Fabiano, Tom Casey, Mel Koich, Dennis Highland, John Matus, Larry O'brien, Bart Pitzer, Len Santoro, John Sullivan, and John Vogt. They all came that first year and are responsible for the structure that is still in place. Their names may not be on the door but their hearts are in that structure. They are giving, sharing, producers that bought into the essence of what the organization is about and yes, they all had confidence in their own ability to succeed. They chased excellence and in doing so, created something amazing.

Our business was built from the ground up, the street if you will, because individual salespeople, in their effort to self-actualize and chase excellence, extended themselves beyond the norm. And at the end of the day, it is the broker, not the corporate hierarchy, who finds success for him or herself. It happens on the streets first and then they move higher and higher up the chain, chasing excellence and their own capabilities, sharing their success, and never, ever stopping.

God bless the broker!

PLATFORM PROFILE
Jim Snyder (Lee & Associates)

Jim is an industrial real estate street broker in Orange County, California in the Newport Beach office for Lee & Associates. Jim has been the top salesperson (number one or two) in that office for twenty-five years. His organization, preparedness, and knowledge lay the groundwork with his unassuming, but direct, personality for a relationship-building juggernaut in his area of influence. Almost no deal gets done without his knowledge in that marketplace.

Jim has enjoyed great success in commercial real estate for a variety of reasons. First and foremost, however, is his consistent, every-day approach to prospecting. He has done it for so long that the process no longer feels like prospecting, but like relationship building, because he has been talking to a majority of the same people for years even though he may not have done a transaction with them. He has passed that difficult period with most of his contacts of having to explain who he is and what he wants. Instead, his calls are familiar and more often than not, welcomed.

A team builder who delegates and utilizes his strengths to maintain dominance in his market, Jim is the all-time sales leader in industrial real estate sales and leasing for Lee & Associates. It's been said of Jim, a former lead tennis player at the University of California at Irvine and professional tennis player, that Jim works his territory as Michael Chang used to work the baseline in his tennis matches. Jim, by the way, defeated Michael both in college and in the professional ranks.

Jim is that broker who started, learned, and built a business plan, every day, a day at a time, in a Southern California industrial market, which is the largest sector market in the world. He has achieved such dominance in his area of expertise that I can think of no other, out of maybe 2,000 industrial practitioners, who can match his success over such a significant period of time. He is a family man, father of two, a leader in his community and his church, and a role model to his peers.

A FINAL THOUGHT

Chasing excellence is a full time endeavor, and while it never stops, it can also become such a routine that it is nothing to fear. At the end of the day, the sense of self-satisfaction that you feel in this chase is such an elixir that you cannot wait for the next day to begin.

Hopefully our stories have demonstrated to you not only the accessibility of excellence, but also the joys of achieving to the best of your ability. When you feel others doubt or criticize your drive, remember to believe in yourself and your commitment to succeed. When mistakes are made, learn from them, and understand that they are part of the excellence process.

Hold on to the passion that gets you up in the morning. When you feel that fire, that's when you know you are in a good spot. And when you don't, that's when you know it's time for a change. At the end of this book, take a serious and honest evaluation of how the chapters made you feel. Fired up? Anxious? Doubtful? Maybe you're shaking your head thinking we're crazy. But we're okay with being a little crazy. Chasing excellence to your fullest extent is a little crazy. Many times it's that bit of crazy, out-of-the-box daring that you need to change your whole world.

Remember too the six platform profiles that you read about. Did you realize that all six of those individuals achieved excellence in a different manner? Coppola challenges life in all of its aspects and fully integrates excellence into the fiber of his being and his local office brokerage platform. Cushman integrates his excellence at the highest level of a national office platform, now going international, with a 365-day focus. Longo leveraged her excellence from an individual local industrial platform into a national institutional sales team platform. Silk leveraged his excellence from a local industrial platform to an innovative national, going international, capital markets institutional sales platform. Snyder continues to leverage his local industrial platform, incrementally, a day at a time, broadening his reach every year. Staubach leveraged his celebrity and leadership qualities with a vision of the future for a client-service platform, and then realized that it was one thing to have the idea and another to implement the idea.

A few final take aways: know the difference between being a salesperson and being a real estate person; one thinks short term and the other thinks long term. Know your greatest strength and spend the majority of your time using it. Know your greatest weakness; deal with it and get back to thinking long term and experiencing joy and satisfaction by doing what you do best.

We have been, and continue to be, very blessed to be in the commercial real estate brokerage industry. From the people we meet to the opportunities we have, every day is a gift. We have so much passion and gratitude for this industry, and look forward to watching the brokers in it grow and succeed. Nothing would make us happier than to know some of the thoughts in this book have helped the reader realize that he, or she, has it in them to be all that they can be and to initiate or further that process.

ABOUT THE AUTHORS

Bill Lee has had an illustrious career in Commercial Real Estate that spans nearly four decades. He began in the business in 1970 at Grubb & Ellis as a transactional broker, winning many company sales awards while also serving as the salesman's representative to the Board of Directors. In 1979, he founded Lee & Associates, a commercial real estate company with a dynamic new business model. The company was, and continues to be, owned equally by its transaction shareholders, a concept that created a sense of shared responsibility and cooperation throughout the organization. Today, Lee & Associates is the fourth largest real estate sales organization in the country, with 54 offices, over 900 brokers and 450 equal owners. Bill oversaw much of this tremendous growth before retiring in 2008 to pursue his hobbies of surfing, gardening, owning a bed and breakfast, and spending time with family and friends.

R. Craig Coppola is the top-producing Broker in Lee & Associates' 36-plus-year history. He is also one of the eight Founding Principals of Lee & Associates Arizona. He holds the three most coveted designations in the industry: CCIM, CRE, and SIOR. He has been a 23-time top producer at Lee & Associates, 6-time NAIOP Office Broker of the year, and an additional 16-time finalist for NAIOP Office Broker of the Year. He is also the author of three additional books, *How to Win in Commercial Real Estate Investing*, *The Art of Commercial Real Estate Leasing*, and *The Fantastic Life*. Outside of the office, Craig is an avid backpacker, husband, and father to four remarkable children.